The **Inner** Matrix

A Guide to Transforming Your Life and Awakening Your Spirit

JOEY KLEIN

BALBOA.
PRESS
A DIVISION OF HAY HOUSE

Balboa Press books may be ordered through booksellers or by contacting:

Balboa Press
A Division of Hay House
1663 Liberty Drive
Bloomington, IN 47403
www.balboapress.com
1 (877) 407-4847

Because of the dynamic nature of the Internet, any web addresses or links contained in this book may have changed since publication and may no longer be valid. The views expressed in this work are solely those of the author and do not necessarily reflect the views of the publisher, and the publisher hereby disclaims any responsibility for them.

The author of this book does not dispense medical advice or prescribe the use of any technique as a form of treatment for physical, emotional, or medical problems without the advice of a physician, either directly or indirectly. The intent of the author is only to offer information of a general nature to help you in your quest for emotional and spiritual well-being. In the event you use any of the information in this book for yourself, which is your constitutional right, the author and the publisher assume no responsibility for your actions.

Any people depicted in stock imagery provided by Thinkstock are models, and such images are being used for illustrative purposes only.
Certain stock imagery © Thinkstock.

Print information available on the last page.

ISBN: 978-1-4525-9177-3 (sc)
ISBN: 978-1-4525-9179-7 (hc)
ISBN: 978-1-4525-9178-0 (e)

Library of Congress Control Number: 2014901984

Balboa Press rev. date: 02/12/2016

Until you make the unconscious conscious, it will direct your life and you will call it fate.

—CARL JUNG

CONTENTS

INTRODUCTION

The Power of the Matrix

I am the master of my fate. I am the captain of my soul.

**—WILLIAM ERNEST HENLEY,
IN "INVICTUS"**

W hen I ask people to identify the most important relationship with the greatest impact on their lives, almost everyone points to someone they love deeply, such as a child, spouse, parent, mentor, or best friend. It always comes as a shock when I tell them that their answer is wrong. The truth is that the most important relationship, with the most profound impact on our lives, is the relationship we have with our self.

It is what lives inside our mind, emotions, body, and spirit that creates the matrix of our inner experience. In turn, that inner matrix determines how we process and define our world. We bring our mind, emotions, body, and spirit to the relationships we have with others, and this inner matrix dictates our ability or inability to thrive in those relationships. Through the lens of our mind, emotions, body, and spirit, we process, define, and influence everything that shows up in our lives.

So what does it mean to be in a relationship with our inner matrix? Most of us assume that because we eat, live, and breathe, we understand who we are and know how to *be* in the world. Few of us pause to consider that appropriate training and education are required if we wish to do anything with excellence in this life. Would you allow a neurosurgeon to operate on your brain if she had not been trained? Would you hire a mechanic to fix your car if he had never repaired a car? Would you hire an attorney who had never been to law school to represent you in court? We can easily imagine that the outcome of any of these situations would be potentially disastrous.

Most of us do not seek to train our inner matrix despite the fact that it defines our quality of life and the level of success we achieve.

We simply do not realize that we can train all aspects of our being, instead believing we are born the way we are. We believe that we either have an inner matrix that creates peace, well-being, and success in life, or we don't. However, the truth is that if we are taught the skills and tools to master our inner matrix, we can shift and change our mental, emotional, physical, and spiritual state to align with any vision we have for our lives. When we learn how to align our inner matrix with any vision we choose, in that moment, our vision instantly becomes our reality. If we wish to create a life of love, peace, and joy, we can do so. All we truly need is to master the skills necessary to be in this world in a state of excellence. When we engage such training, we can begin to consciously evolve our inner matrix in a way that serves us to reach our highest potential in life.

Almost all of us have an area in our lives that is not functioning on an optimal level or where some amount of pain and suffering shows up. Perhaps we have a relationship where conflict is present. It may be a job where we believe our skills are not being appropriately utilized. Our finances may be a source of struggle from time to time. Even when all is right in the world, we may just have a sense that a deeper, more fulfilling experience is possible.

No matter what level we are functioning on, most of us have an intuitive knowing that we can develop ourselves beyond our current state. For many of us, we have just not found the tools we were looking for to create the life we know is possible. The good news is that this book provides the opportunity to gain practical and easy-to-apply tools that can facilitate true transformation in any aspect of life. By learning to shift the mind, emotions, physical body, and spirit we simply gain the power to change every experience we have in this world.

If our mind is disciplined, our emotions are peaceful, and our physicality is strong, we will have one experience of the world. If our mind is chaotic, our emotions are frenzied, and our physical body is weak, our experience of that exact same world will be radically different. Although we have long recognized that we can strengthen a weak human body, not everyone understands that we can train all aspects of our internal life, including the mind, emotions, physical body, and spirit. When we change these inner aspects, the world interacts with us differently. Therefore, if we wish to shape our relationships with family, friends, coworkers, humanity, and the world at large, the first place that we must look is inside ourselves.

When we were born, very few of us received an instruction manual for our inner matrix. We were not trained to look inside and optimize our state of being. We were not educated about the impact our internal state of being has on the quality of experiences we create in this world. Instead, the random set of experiences we encountered in this life conditioned our mind, emotions, and physical bodies to react to our environment in certain specific ways. As a result, we operate in our lives without fully understanding who we are or how we function. We also fail to grasp the true extent of the influence we have on the world around us, as well as the influence the world has on us.

In order to truly thrive in our lives, we must first understand how we work, and to do that we must build a relationship with our inner matrix. Having gained this understanding, we can then execute the necessary changes to eliminate our current areas of suffering, define our dreams and visions, and create an extraordinary life. Without such education and training, our lives become chaotic and painful. We are left to wonder how we ended up in a place of mental, emotional, and physical turmoil, without hope for escape.

I did not grow up in an environment saturated in peace, love, and joy. What looked like a rather idyllic middle-class, suburban world had its fair share of anger, conflict, resentment, pain, and suffering. As I approached my teenage years, I began to focus on how I would chart my own destiny in this life. When I looked at those around me, I was aware that although these people experienced moments of happiness, no one seemed to be at peace within themselves or living a fulfilled life. When they did experience happiness, it was only as a result of something that had showed up in their outside world. Lacking the skills to manage their internal states, they were forced to look to their outside environments to trigger the internal experience they desired.

My parents, siblings, aunts, uncles, friends, religious leaders, and even teachers seemed generally dissatisfied with their lives. For example, nothing would excite my dad more than the prospect of a new job. He would convince himself that a new company or a new position at work would make all the difference for him. However, a few months after obtaining his new job, my dad would again be complaining about his boss, how much he was getting paid, and the work he had to perform. In no time at all, he would want to leave the job he had been so excited to obtain.

For my mom, she would be happy when her family and friends would come to visit. Once they left, she would slip back into a state of general depression, watching television, reading a book, and basically detaching from her world. My mother lived an isolated and lonely existence despite the fact that she had a husband and children who loved her and desperately hungered for her attention. My mother was trapped, unable to experience the beauty that was right in front of her, available for her own taking.

My teachers did not seem fulfilled either. They appeared to just be working a job as opposed to having a true passion for their vocation. Something was missing. Even my best friend's mom was no different. Although she would be elated when she got a new car, the angry face she typically displayed for the world would quickly return. The external circumstances she thought would bring her happiness, failed time and time again to create the lasting experience she yearned for in this life.

I was raised in a family with two religions: my mother was Catholic and my father was Jewish. As the time for my bar mitzvah approached, my father insisted that I attend countless hours of Hebrew school. I secretly hoped that my synagogue would lead me to a place of peace, love, and joy. However, this religious experience failed to offer me a way out. As I asked increasingly inquisitive questions about life, my rabbi, who lacked the answers himself, often became angry and would punish me.

He would attempt to shame me, telling me I should have faith and obey. No questioning was allowed.

The people surrounding me reiterated a broader societal message to me about how to live a happy life. The message was to go to college, get a well-paying job, find a nice girl, and have a family of my own. In other words, I needed to do exactly what those around me had done and then I would reach the promised land. The problem was that I did not want to grow up to have their experiences of life. I had the sense that if I took their advice, that was exactly where I would end up. As a result, I was very hesitant to follow in the footsteps of those whom I knew.

I had been born with a level of awareness that those around me did not appear to share. I saw my parents and the adults I knew repeatedly engage in the same patterns of behavior that did not serve their highest or best interests. I knew they were trapped in these patterns, unable to choose a different way of being in the world. I could not understand why they engaged in the same behavioral patterns over and over again, each time thinking that this time, they would get a different result.

I began to feel like I was trapped in my own version of Bill Murray's *Groundhog Day*. In that movie, the central character repeats the same day over and over again with the same disappointing and painful results. In the movie, the character actually realizes that he is trapped and repeating the same failed behavior causing the same disastrous outcomes; whereas those around me seemed to be slumbering through their lives, believing that they were exercising choice in the world when they were actually the architects of their own conditioned prison.

Conversely, I carried a deep conviction that there was simply a better way to be in this world, though I had never been shown an example of what that could look like. I believed that my relationships should be harmonious. I was convinced it was possible to live in states of peace and serenity. I knew that unconditional love was possible. I hungered for a deep and ever-present connection to spirit. The problem was that I did not know how to show up in such capacities, and I had never met anyone who did.

Although I had not found a guide for my journey, as soon as I was able, I set out to pave my own road in the world. I was determined to live a life quite different from what I had seen around me. My best friend and I moved out of our parents' homes, got an apartment together with our girlfriends, and entered a very rebellious time. At first there was a sense of freedom and excitement about the promise this new existence held. We had rejected society's fantasy-recipe for happiness, and instead, we were creating something better. We were committed to doing things differently and living happily ever after.

Quickly, our venture turned into something we had neither intended nor anticipated. Our new world became a chaotic existence filled with more pain and suffering then I had ever known—even more than in the path I was rebelling against. In a short period of time, I learned that awareness of what was wrong with my life did not provide a solution. Soon I found myself working a meaningless job during the day and partying at night. It was not long before hopelessness and despair filled my inner world. In an attempt to avoid the pain, I began to numb myself. My life became filled with drugs and alcohol. My girlfriend and I broke up, and my relationship with my best friend dissolved into conflict.

In the life I had sought to escape, I had known anger, resentment, depression, pain, and suffering, but not at these levels, which had escalated to the point of excruciating. Although I was aware of the patterns my parents had engaged in and the pain they had created for themselves, to my dismay, I found myself engaging in the same patterns I had intended to step away from. My heightened sense of awareness seemed only to have amplified my level of suffering and the speed at which I encountered it. It had done nothing to create the different life I had intended. My life had become unbearable.

Eventually, I found myself at rock bottom. A night of partying began like any other, but this time, I began to spiral out of control. I was drinking heavily and doing drugs. One night turned into three. With no food or sleep, I began to hallucinate. In the middle of the third night, I was watching a movie with friends, when all of a sudden, a band of dancing bears appeared in the living room! I was thrilled to see them and could not figure out why everyone else was missing this amazing opportunity to dance with bears.

At some point, however, I noticed the horrified looks on my friends' faces and excused myself to go to my room and try to sleep. After a while, I tried to get up to get a drink of water but couldn't move my body. I became aware that the sound of my heartbeat was slowing down. Soon, I found myself above my body looking down at my resting form in the bed. I heard a voice say, "We don't have time to build another vehicle. We have to fix this one." Suddenly I was back in my body.

By morning, I had made a decision. I knew beyond a shadow of a doubt that if I stayed in my current environment, I would be dead soon. I also knew that I had not come to this life to live in an alcohol-and-drug-induced haze. On the other hand, I had no intention of leading a mundane or meaningless existence either. I believed that I was here to accomplish something more. I was in a place of decision that would lead me to a radical transformation. So much for my happily-ever-after fantasy; for now, it was back to my parents' basement.

Home with my parents, I entered a time of deep, internal reflection. Over and over I asked, *What is my purpose? Who am I? And Why am I here?* For months, I isolated myself from the outside world and dove deeper into the depths of my inner matrix. Far from feeling defeated, I became more determined than ever to find the answers, heal my inner world, and ultimately reach a place of fulfillment. Armed with that determination and the painful lessons learned, I set out to find real teachers who could show me another way of being in this life.

Ultimately, this journey brought me to an unexpected place: a teacher from India. The moment I met my teacher, I experienced a sense of deep and profound recognition. She was at once all-powerful and all-loving, fierce and gentle, peaceful and yet fully expressive in the moment. Before me sat the example of unconditional love that I had believed was possible but had almost given up on finding in this life. Although I knew almost nothing about her tradition or culture, I immediately knew that the *presence* she carried was what I had been searching for and something I wished to devote my life to awakening within myself. Sitting in a room with several hundred other attendees, I realized that she had the capacity to guide me to a new way of being. I knew this teacher would show me what it was to truly live. For the first time, I had a taste of what was possible.

My teacher brought with her an eclectic background, steeped in mystical Eastern tradition and yoga as well as Western psychology. She had practiced as a therapist in France for years. She was trained in naturopathic, homeopathic, and osteopathic therapies and had enjoyed an extensive health-and-wellness practice. Although she had risen to the highest rank ever awarded a woman in 2,700 years of Vedic tradition, at the time I met her, she was relatively unknown in the United States. Pulling on this vast and varied training, she was capable of guiding people through deep transformation and could eliminate extreme suffering of all kinds. Although traditional Western thought teaches us that such profound change takes years of therapy if not a lifetime, she often created such transformation in a matter of hours or even minutes. I was in awe.

As I dived into the work with my teacher, she brought me to a place where I could see that my outer world was a reflection of my inner matrix and that if I wanted to change my experience of life, I had to change myself. As I continued with her work and took accountability for my life, in a short period of time, my entire world shifted on a deep and profound level.

I moved from extreme suffering to a place of authentic peace and well-being inside of myself. It no longer mattered what happened around me. Now I was able to maintain states of peace and joy despite what showed up in my life. Although I did not understand how these changes were possible, everything in my life had shifted in a relatively short period of time. Those around me were also transforming in ways that I could not explain. Even my parents were changing. My father stopped complaining and actually began enjoying his work. My mother finally found a sense of joy in her life. Seeing these radical transformations, I knew I had found my life's work.

Over time, my teacher asked me to share what I had learned with others. It was not long before I had a thriving private-coaching practice with sixty people on my books and a long waiting list. Because I could only accommodate a limited number of clients in private practice and my wait list was growing longer with each passing week, I began offering weekend seminars to bring these practices to a wider audience. Ultimately, these programs grew to my teaching over thirty seminars a year in cities across the United States.

During this same time, I discovered a traditional Korean martial-arts school in Los Angeles, California, that taught me the importance of developing the physical body in relationship to one's internal life. Through intense study, I learned how to face fear by entering the ring as a warrior. This skill translated outside of the martial-arts studio and into my daily life. As a result of this practice, I discovered the importance of discipline and how to cultivate true inner strength. Teaching at the martial-arts studio, known as a *dojang*, I developed critical leadership skills rooted in a tradition thousands of years old. Recognizing the value these ancient skills and traditions had to offer, I set out to fully embody them.

In Beverly Hills, I met a highly regarded psychologist whose clients included many of Hollywood's high-profile figures in film and music. This psychologist began to mentor me and ultimately invited me to coach many of her clients. As a result of my work with her, I became intrigued by the world of science and what Western research has discovered about internal development. I began to read books about psychology, neuroplasticity, and epigenetics. Although the field of psychology has been around for over a century, neuroplasticity and epigenetics are relatively new scientific arenas addressing how the brain can be rewired and our genetic expression altered by activities such as mindfulness meditation. I desired to understand, from a scientific standpoint, why I had been able to achieve such radical changes in my life through employing the principals I had learned from my other teachers. These emerging areas of research offered the explanation I had sought to find. The information I discovered deepened my understanding of inner transformational work and emerging areas of science that now support many of these ancient traditions.

In the course of this work, I learned that we no longer have to guess at how to empower ourselves. The research and scientific support for how to step into strong and fulfilling lives exists, but a relatively small amount of that work has been summarized and distributed to a mainstream audience. I knew that one of my lifelong goals would be to merge the areas of ancient mystical practices and modern scientific development to revolutionize the work of inner transformation.

While living in Los Angeles, I also met a Kabbalistic rabbi who took me deep into the world of ancient Jewish mysticism. Unlike my childhood rabbi who punished my questioning because he lacked the answers, this wise Kabbalist encouraged me to question and expertly directed me on a path to discover the answers I had sought for myself. I became a devoted private student of his and studied with him for years. In the end, I gained a deep appreciation for the beauty that lies in our great wisdom traditions when we have an experienced guide who can take us beyond the dogma and into the profound and limitless experience of spirit.

During my vast and varied training, I found myself challenging the methods our society has long offered as solutions to our human suffering and guidance for transforming our lives. For example, many have been to a therapist or coach and were taught that if we are aware of what we are doing and why we are doing it, then we can change ourselves for the better. Unfortunately, awareness of a problem does not define a solution. A lyric from a popular 1980s song, *The Policy of Truth* by Depeche Mode perfectly summarizes the experience that almost everyone has had in life: "Never again is what you swore the time before." We see what we are doing. We vow to change and never to do it again. We hold the best of intentions. Then, to our dismay, we find ourselves engaging in the same destructive behavior over and over.

Far from providing a solution, what neurologists have now discovered is that when we think about a pattern we wish to change, neurologically that pattern gets stronger. Because the brain functions in the same way a muscle does, the more exercise any pathway receives, the stronger it becomes. When we think about how we feel and try to discover the reasons for why we feel a certain way, we are engaging the neurological connections for the patterns we are trying to escape. Instead of eliminating the pattern, it grows stronger. As a result, thinking our way out of a problem simply fails.

The other popular suggestion for how to guide our lives out of suffering is to follow our gut instincts. A common misperception is that our intuition lives in our gut and if we follow its guidance, things will get better. As scientists in the emerging field of neurogastroenterology have discovered, a large portion of our emotions actually live in our gut. The gut is often referred to as our *second brain*. However, this *second brain* does not control any higher intellectual functioning. Instead, our gut's neurological purpose is a site for emotional patterning. We all have felt butterflies in our stomach when we were anxious. We have all experienced an emotional situation that was so intense, it made our stomach hurt. Science now understands that the reason we have these common experiences is that some of our emotional neurology lives in our gut.

When we follow our gut, instead of accessing higher-level intuition, we are actually accessing our lower, often times destructive, emotional patterns. Because we have engaged these emotional patterns our entire lives on some level, they actually feel comfortable. In fact, they feel *right* to us. As a result, we mistake this feeling of familiarity as some intuitive sign that we are on the right path. Instead, we are on the same path that ends up taking us to the same place of familiar suffering. When we don't understand that we are accessing our emotions instead of our spirit or higher intuition, we are left wondering how spirit could have failed us.

Through my journey into the inner matrix, I not only realized what wasn't working, but I also began to synthesize certain fundamental principles that were transforming the lives of my private clients and the students at my seminars. I drew my teachings from the wide and varied traditions, both modern and ancient, that I had studied and developed a system known as *Conscious Transformation*. Through these methods, I transformed my own life and showed people how to consciously transform their lives on all levels. This system of Conscious Transformation empowers individuals to become the architect of their lives, giving them practical tools to intentionally create any vision they choose.

People who were on the brink of divorce developed stable and loving relationships with their partners. Those who faced professional challenges discovered career success and thrived financially. Clients who suffered from serious and even debilitating physical illnesses shifted into states of health and vibrancy. Over and over again, my clients were learning that it was not necessary for them to suffer in this life, and armed with the tools I gave them, they were stepping out of pain and into states of joy and bliss. Through the practice of Conscious Transformation, profound changes were coming in a matter of months, weeks, and sometimes, even days. In this book, I seek to share my discoveries with you.

So why has this work been effective at addressing such varied issues and situations? Romantic relationships, families, physical health, businesses, and careers are all based on a single foundation: the relationship with the inner matrix. This internal relationship is the most important relationship we have, and it is the most overlooked. It is the topic about which we receive the least education, but it is the one where we should receive the most. Although the ancients knew this truth, our popular culture seems to have lost sight of this great wisdom. When you master your internal state, you master your world. It is just that simple.

The world is full of examples of how those who master their internal states are capable of looking tragedies in the face and thriving, while those who do not are crippled by life's challenges. World-famous physicist and author Stephen Hawking, who was diagnosed with ALS when he was twenty-one and not expected to live beyond the age of twenty-three is a good example. Hawking says, "I try to lead as normal a life as possible and not think about my condition or regret the things it prevents me from doing, which are not many." Now in his seventies, Hawking, who is married with three children, has not been able to walk or talk for decades, but his work as head of the Center for Theoretical Cosmology at Cambridge has literally changed the way humanity sees the universe and our place in it.

On the other hand, when we do not master ourselves and difficult challenges show up, those moments define us, permanently transforming our lives into something we did not intend. A client of mine is an attorney who built a national law practice representing those who suffer severe burn injuries. For twenty-five years, she has seen example after example of how a split-second can chart the course of our lives when we allow it.

This attorney has watched her clients' lives disintegrate after a catastrophic injury. Otherwise functional individuals simply cannot find the strength to go on. Her clients slip into depression, anxiety, and often prescription-drug addiction. Marriages and entire families are routinely destroyed as grief, anger, and regret consume those affected by these misfortunes. Parents who have lost children frequently suffer severe and even deadly physical illness, not to mention levels of trauma so deep that suicide seems the only way out. When unprepared for the dark night of the soul that comes for us all, that darkness can be all consuming.

One of the reasons this attorney became involved with my work was that, for the first time, she saw a system that could empower people to face even life's most daunting challenges. Having watched so many be crippled by life's experiences, she sought to be a force capable of influencing the world instead of one who was crushed by external circumstances. At my programs, she witnessed students of mine developing internal discipline that allowed them to face their most terrifying inner demons and thrive when most would crumble. Through my teachings, she learned how to make an impact on her own world instead of allowing the tragedy surrounding her professional life to impact her. The potential to be a force in this world instead of a prisoner to it is a gift I offer to you.

When we are taught basic skills for mastering our inner matrix, we become the force that influences the world instead of the victim of what shows up in our lives. In our day-to-day existence, we are able to bring meaning and purpose to even the most mundane tasks. In what would otherwise be devastating situations, we suddenly see the power of potential staring back at us. Armed with tools to train our internal state, we are able to master our destiny even in the face of life's most formidable storms.

* * *

To begin training your internal state, first read the book in its entirety before doing the practices contained within. The book contains the knowledge you need to train your internal matrix. At the end of the book, you will find a strategy guide providing the practices for creating Conscious Transformation. Through these practices, you apply the book's teachings to your life. Transformation requires both knowledge and application. Application requires consistent practice. Knowledge alone is useless if you do not apply that knowledge to your life. My goal is not just to inform you but to empower you.

While you engage this book, I challenge you to temporarily drop your preconceived ideas of who you are, how you function, and what it is that will take you out of suffering and into a new state of being. As Socrates noted, "an unexamined life is not worth living." Dive into your inner world. Set the intention to stay open to learning about your inner matrix. Entertain the idea that perhaps the world and your place in it is not exactly as you might have believed it to be in the past. If you're willing to drop your current worldview and allow yourself to temporarily entertain the possibility of an alternative one, a grand journey into the inner depths of your magnificent being will emerge. If you engage this quest fully, you will discover who you truly are and a radical new way of existing in this world that empowers you to choose the experiences you wish to create.

Having the courage to embark upon a journey to examine what lives in your inner matrix and the determination to see this adventure through with humor is critical if you wish to experience transformation. However, in the end, what I am offering you is a no-risk proposition. If you choose to become committed to taking the journey into the inner matrix with me, a new experience of the human existence and all you have sensed was possible lies on this path. If you choose not to engage a new way of being, your old existence will still be waiting for you.

In the course of my practice, I have worked with individuals from all socioeconomic backgrounds, religions, cultures, and ethnicities. All have benefited from the practices of Conscious Transformation and its easy-to-use tools to empower a modern society. Throughout this book, I share with you stories of transformation from a number of my clients who experienced radical change. Their names and certain identifying details have been changed to protect their privacy.

These techniques, which I will share with you, can be applied to your daily life so that you can create an extraordinary existence by learning how to navigate yourself and, at the same time, begin to understand the science supporting these empowering practices. Once you learn how to be the architect of your mind, emotions, and physical body, and have the power to access your spiritual intuition, radical transformation will unfold throughout your entire life.

Although we have been told that such radical transformation takes a long time, the truth is it doesn't have to take years, months, or even weeks. Stepping out of pain and suffering, opening ourselves to all that is possible in this human experience and, thereby, completely transforming all aspects of ourselves does not have to be a lifetime affair. Transformation always happens in just one moment. This book will show you how to create that moment.

CHAPTER 1

The First Relationships

Everything that we see is a shadow cast by that which we do not see.

—MARTIN LUTHER KING, JR.

We often associate the term *relationship* with the connection we have to a spouse, lover, or family member. In truth, we are actually in relationship with everything outside of ourselves. We are in relationship with friends, acquaintances, jobs, houses, cars, and even the person who cuts us off in traffic. The very fabric of our lives is woven through the lens of relationship.

Our inner matrix and the level of consciousness we embody define the experience that we have of each relationship in our lives. Most people think that the people or things in their outside world determine their experiences in life. Our society teaches that if we have the right relationship, the right house, and the right job, all will be well. As a result, we try moving the pieces on our external checkerboards to get all of the pieces in the right places. When this fails to make us happy, we think we have the wrong pieces on our board, so we change the people, places, or things in our lives.

We believe our external world is the cause of our unhappiness, because we cannot see our internal state of being. The truth is, it is extremely difficult to see ourselves, without the right internal training and tools. Because we are unable to see inside ourselves, we can't change what we can't see. To see our inner matrix and how it creates every aspect of our lives, we need powerful techniques. When equipped with the right tools, relationships serve as a type of inner telescope, enabling us to see what lies deep within and to facilitate Conscious Transformation. When we transform in this profound way, our experience of life and the relationships in our lives will radically improve.

Each time we engage someone in a relationship, an energy exists between the two of us. Although most of us have limited knowledge about this phenomenon, on an intuitive level, we know it to be true. In describing relationships, we even use common phrases that evoke a sense of this energetic presence. When two people are attracted to each other, we talk in terms of the "electricity" between them. When anger exists between two people, we often hear someone comment "you could cut the tension with a knife." Most of us have been to a funeral or a hospital where people were grieving and heard the sadness described as "hanging in the air."

So what accounts for our tangible experience of this intangible element of relationship? In such situations, we simply sense the energy that is the building block of everything in our world. Physics now teaches that everything in existence is made up of vibrating strings of energy. The only differentiation among these strings of energy is with regard to how each string vibrates and its rate of vibration. Quantum physics refers to this concept as *string theory*. On our most elemental level, human beings are merely strings of vibrating energy in empty space. Even our thoughts and emotions are actually vibrating energy. These vibrating strings or waves of energy are the building blocks of consciousness.

All living things, from plants to animals, are conscious on some level or another, but not all living things are self-aware. For example, although a tiger is conscious, it takes action from a place of instinct, not a place of awareness. A tiger does not know that it is a tiger. A tiger is not self-aware. A tiger takes action based upon its nature through instinct; it cannot change its nature or its instinct. A tiger will always do what a tiger is designed to do. It does not stop to analyze whether it is morally appropriate to kill a gazelle. If it is hungry, it follows its instinct and feeds its hunger. It does not ponder whether it should have grass or gazelle. A tiger eats what a tiger eats.

Human beings are conscious, but we are also self-aware. We can identify that we are human. We can perceive our own thoughts, our emotions, and the sensations in our bodies. We have the ability to question our own existence and aspire to evolve beyond our current state. Through awareness, we can alter our level of consciousness by shifting how we think, how we feel, and the condition of our bodies. The level of consciousness that we embody as human beings defines our experience of life and our capacity to influence the world around us. When armed with the right tools, we can create our environments instead of allowing our environments to influence and impact us.

In order to elevate our level of consciousness and expand our ability to be self-aware, we must first understand how our level of consciousness came to be what it is today. The key is to explore our inner matrix. Once we understand how our inner matrix was developed, we gain access to how that matrix functions within us and the impact it has on the world around us. Expanding our awareness is the first step to consciously transforming our lives.

As we discussed, the inner matrix is comprised of four separate yet interrelated bodies. These are the mental, emotional, and physical bodies and a fourth body that we refer to as the spiritual body. The spiritual body is the part of us that extends beyond our human existence. We discover the inner matrix within the intricate facets of our minds, the vast expressions that we call our emotions, the intoxicating sensations we experience in the body, and the infinite, divine mystery that is our spiritual self. We expand our awareness of the inner matrix by looking within and having the courage to explore the vast creation that exists inside each and every one of us. If we wish to realize our full potential and go beyond the mundane experience of life, we must be willing to master our mind, emotions, and physical body, and increase our opening to spirit.

As a starting point for understanding how we develop, it is important to acknowledge that everything that exists in this universe existed as something else before it took its current form. Before a plant became a plant, an animal became an animal, a human became a human, and the world became our beloved planet, each existed as pure, formless energy or *Presence*. This Presence then took form and became a tree, an animal, a human, or the very world we inhabit. It is this same energy that gives us the ability to feel, to think, and to have sensation in the body. Before we were in our physical forms experiencing human consciousness, we too existed as formless energy.

At the time of conception, this pure, formless energy entered the wombs of our mothers. Although we were just molecules and cells coming into form, these molecules and cells embodied consciousness. A level of intelligence existed in these molecules and cells that held the blueprint for who we were to become. In this initial moment we received genetic and epigenetic coding from both our mother and our father. The *epigenome* is like a switch that sits on top of the gene and is affected by environmental triggers, including stress and trauma. An event occurs in our external environment and that event causes the epigenetic switch to turn the gene on, turn it off, or increase or decrease the intensity with which the gene expresses itself. Such changes in the epigenome are now understood to be passed from one generation to the next. Through the epigenome, a multitude of information is passed from parent to child including emotional programming.

In a study from Emory University, scientists taught male mice to fear the smell of cherry-blossoms by associating the smell with mild foot shocks over a period of three days. Later the mice bred and both their children and grandchildren feared the smell of cherry blossoms even though the resulting generations had never been shocked in response to this smell. The offspring were even born with more cherry-blossom detecting neurons in their noses and more space in their brain devoted to cherry-blossom smelling. As the Washington Post noted, this study "adds to a growing pile of evidence suggesting that characteristics outside of the strict genetic code may also be acquired from our parents through epigenetic inheritance." In other words, science is now proving that fear and other learned emotional expressions are imprinted at an epigenetic level and passed from one generation to the next.

Once we were in utero, our mother's environment began to impact our epigenetic settings having the ability to turn these switches on and off. Because our physicality was attached to our mother's in this initial stage, we began to experience what our mother was experiencing through her patterns of vibrating energy. Our mother's world was our world. As our mother felt emotions, these energetic patterns began to imprint into our developing emotional body. As our mother had thoughts, beliefs, and concepts run through her mind, our developing mind was energetically imprinted with these patterns of information. As our mother experienced physical sensations, our forming physical body was imprinted with this information as well. In fact, all that we could experience at that point was our mother's experiences passed on to us as information through patterns of vibrating energy. This is why our relationship with our mother was the most powerful and influential relationship.

As any builder will tell you, nothing is more important to a structure than the foundation on which it is built. While we were in our mother's womb, we did not have developed mental, emotional, or physical bodies. The patterns of vibrating energy that we received from our mother's experiences laid the foundation for how our mind, body, and emotions would function throughout our lives. Our very first experiences of being human were experienced through our mothers. This first relationship with our mother clearly defined how we would be in relationship with ourselves, with others, and with the world in general.

This first relationship exerts a power in development that is still not fully appreciated in our modern society but is becoming more and more recognized by our scientific community. The topic of the mother's impact upon her developing child is tackled in a well-regarded book written by three preeminent psychiatrists, Thomas Lewis, Fari Amini and Richard Lannon entitled *A General Theory of Love*. In this book, the authors reconcile ancient beliefs with what science has now learned about the function and construction of the human brain. In doing so, they recognize that we have a deep need for love, even in our earliest moments, and that our neurological development is directly affected by whether we receive love during those earliest moments in human form.

These authors conclude that scientific research shows that our nervous systems, and our brains in particular, are not self-contained. Instead, from these earliest moments inside our mother's womb, our brains actually *link* with those of the people close to us in a rhythm that physically imprints the very structure of our brains and influences our functioning for the rest of our lives. In this way, our mother's experiences literally shape our own.

These imprints from our mothers construct lifelong emotional patterns. These emotional patterns then chart the course of our lives. When we don't receive essential emotional patterning such as love, which our brains require for healthy development, we spend our lives trying to "fill in" that empty place. We look to relationships outside of ourselves. Sometimes we numb our pain through unhealthy external means such as drugs, alcohol, food, sex, or other types of mood-altering behavior.

Several years ago, I had an opportunity to witness firsthand a community that appreciates the essential fact that we all need to be loved in order to blossom. I was invited to speak at a United Nations conference on peace in Bangkok, Thailand. While I was there, I stayed for three weeks as a guest at a Buddhist ashram.

Every morning around nine o'clock, approximately forty pregnant women would come and sit for several hours with the Buddhist monk who presided over the ashram. When I asked what was happening, it was explained to me that these women had been raped, abused, or abandoned by their babies' fathers. The monk was teaching the mothers how to love, care for, and nurture their unborn children, despite their difficult situations.

These monks understood that the thoughts, emotions, and sensations that these mothers had about their unborn children as well as the world around them would mold and imprint the mental, emotional, and physical bodies of their children. In fact, these very thoughts, emotions, and physical sensations would become the building blocks upon which the children's inner matrixes would be constructed. This foundation would then determine the overall state of well-being for each child. The monks knew that during these initial moments of our existence in utero, we are imprinted with mental, emotional, and physical patterns that exert a powerful force defining the trajectory of the rest of our lives.

For example, we can imagine the feelings that we would have if we were a mother who had become pregnant as the result of a rape or other traumatic experience. We would most likely have feelings of horror, disgust, shame, worthlessness, anger, guilt, regret, rage, and humiliation. Those emotions would then fuel certain thoughts like *every time I look at my child, I will think of what happened,* or *how can I possibly tell my child how he or she came to be?* These thoughts and emotions would cause physical expressions to follow. Our hearts would race or ache. Our bodies would most likely feel tight, constricted, tired, and even painful.

Perhaps we would be forced to take on multiple jobs just to support ourselves. We might even be living in an abusive environment. Such situations cause enormous mental, emotional, physical, and spiritual trauma. We would be directly affected by each experience of fear, exhaustion, pain, and lack.

In turn, our unborn child would also have the experience of each one of our thoughts, emotions, and physical sensations. As we have discussed, these thoughts, emotions, and physical sensations create energetic imprints on our developing children, thereby shaping each child's emerging inner matrix. Unless attended to, those imprints would last a lifetime. In such a situation, the foundation of the child's developing inner matrix would be laid by patterns created out of a deep level of mental, emotional, and physical suffering. These imprints would carry the information of disgust, shame, worthlessness, anger, regret, rage, and humiliation. In turn, these imprints would cause our children's consciousness to vibrate at the level of disgust, shame, worthlessness, anger, guilt, regret, rage and humiliation.

Research conducted on pregnant women who were either at the World Trade Center during the September 11, 2001, attack or close by confirms that such trauma is actually passed onto children. Researchers at the Traumatic Stress Studies Division of the Mount Sinai Medical Center in New York studied a group of these women and their babies. The mothers who were traumatized by the events of 9/11 were significantly more likely to have babies who showed substantially increased distress in response to loud noises, unfamiliar faces, and new food.

The Mount Sinai researchers concluded that these mothers passed their trauma onto their children through epigenetic means. This research underlies how environmental forces, even when we are in utero have the potential to impact us to the point of our genetic expression. With this scientific understanding of the impact of the experiences we receive in utero, the importance of consciously cultivating a loving experience while a mother is pregnant and its potential effect on current and future generations becomes clear.

These same principles hold true in more positive situations as well. Imagine that while you were pregnant, you had a loving partner, a stable family, and a supportive community. In this situation, you would not have to work a job or be concerned about having good food or shelter. You could be excited about the prospect of being a mother and bringing this child into the world. You would feel supported by your spouse and family in a happy household.

On an emotional level, under these circumstances, you would experience joy, contentment, peace, hope, and love. These feelings would fuel thoughts such as *I am so lucky to be having a baby; I can't wait to be a mother;* or *I look forward to all of the things my husband and I will do with our new child.* In return, these thoughts and emotions would create certain physical sensations. You might feel relaxed, energetic, strong, and vibrant.

All these emotions, thoughts, and physical sensations once again would leave a certain imprint on the developing inner matrix of your unborn child. Later in life, your child would still carry these energetic patterns at its most basic level. These imprints carrying the information of joy, contentment, peace, hope, and love would cause your child's consciousness to vibrate at the level of joy, contentment, peace, hope, and love. These emotional influences, having had an epigenetic impact, could be passed from one generation to the next.

Clearly, we only have the capacity to give an unborn child what we already have ourselves. Mothers can wish for a joyful existence for their children, but if the mother is not experiencing joy, the energetic pattern of joy will not be passed on to the child. If the child does not receive the information of joy, then the child will be unable to create or experience joy within him or herself. Having never received the energetic imprint of joy, the child would not have an active consciousness of joy within.

A child who does not embody an active consciousness of joy is unable to recognize or experience joy when it appears in his or her world. To this child, a pattern of joy would be like someone speaking a foreign language that cannot be understood. The child knows only the language of his or her active emotional patterns, which are determined by the information passed to the child from the mother's experiences. As a result, the first relationship we experience in our life, the relationship with our mother, has a significant bearing on every relationship to follow.

* * *

My client Elizabeth is another highly accomplished attorney who has achieved success in almost every arena she has ever entered. Yet Elizabeth can't accept compliments. They make her uncomfortable. She is highly self-driven and, despite her successes, no accomplishment has ever been enough. Critical comments, on the other hand, Elizabeth hears over and over again in her head for weeks. She beats herself up over the smallest of failings. She has spent her life trying to live up to her own unreasonable expectations, not stopping to enjoy her triumphs but instead moving on toward her next goal.

Elizabeth graduated at the top of her class in law school. She was so focused and concerned about how she would do in her next phase that she started work before she even graduated, instead of taking a little time off with the rest of her peers to enjoy her academic achievement. She thought little about what she had accomplished and instead worried incessantly about whether she would be able to succeed in the competitive law practice she now worked in.

As a young associate, Elizabeth billed more hours to clients than anyone else on her level, but when she received compliments, she could not enjoy them. After she would take a deposition or have a hearing in court, she would play back pieces of those events over and over again in her mind, thinking that she could have done better and experiencing great anxiety, guilt, and shame. When her boyfriend would compliment her on the beautiful dinner she had made, she would think secretly to herself that he didn't really mean it. When someone would tell her how pretty she looked, her mind would go to the weight she needed to lose or the concern that her hair was not perfect.

Elizabeth now has a daughter, Elise. Elise makes straight As and is at the top of her class academically. She published a book at age twelve. She goes to her martial-arts dojo five nights a week and received her black belt a year ahead of schedule. Elise makes self-deprecating comments, just like her mother, in the face of well-earned compliments. She is uncomfortable with praise. She is quietly devastated by what she perceives to be the smallest of criticisms. She is unable to enjoy her successes, because no achievement is quite enough.

Elizabeth was born to an unmarried woman and given up for adoption. Elizabeth lacked the consciousness of healthy self-pride and a feeling of worthiness because her mother did not have those patterns to pass on to her daughter. As a result, Elizabeth spent her life trying to compensate for a general feeling of lack, certain that her next accomplishment would fill that sense of emptiness.

Because Elizabeth didn't hold healthy emotional patterns herself, she was unable to pass them on to her daughter. Despite the fact that Elizabeth wanted desperately for her daughter to experience self-pride, worthiness, and contentment in her life, Elizabeth could not *transmit* an energetic pattern that she did not have. She could only pass on to Elise the same unconscious negative patterns she had absorbed. By working with me to learn the skills to develop her inner matrix, Elizabeth and Elise were able to elevate their levels of consciousness, allowing them to experience the positive states that they had both longed for.

If mothers are aware and know how to create healthier mental, emotional, and physical bodies for themselves, then their unborn children will have access to those same energetic patterns. Therefore, we can easily see how mothers in both negative and positive scenarios could benefit from teachings like those delivered by the Buddhist monk. The monk's teachings would create healthier thoughts, emotions, and physical experiences in the mothers, thereby altering their children's development on a very profound level. I can't think of a mother who would not make such changes, if she understood the importance of her experiences in constructing her child's life and had the tools to create such experiences at will for herself.

The mothers in each of these scenarios are products of their own upbringing and environment, as are we. None of us has access to what we have not experienced and what we have not received. Unless we learn how to expand, shift, and evolve, we will always be limited by the past experiences that have molded our current states of consciousness.

By the time a child is born, a significant amount of imprinting has already occurred within the child's inner matrix. As we have discussed, although we begin as pure energy, we take on a tremendous amount of energetic imprinting from our mother and her surrounding environment while we are in the womb. Therefore, by the time we draw our first breath, we carry these initial ingrained emotional, mental, and physical patterns into our lives.

The moment of birth is our very first experience of being independent and separate from all other things. Although we do not have the mental capacity at that point to understand separateness on an intellectual level, we have the direct experience of suddenly being physically separated from our mother, who had been our entire world. For the first time, we are no longer one with her.

Even though our physical body is now separate from our mother and all other things, on an energetic level, we continue to take on imprints from everyone with whom we come into contact. During infancy, the primary imprints we absorb are those from our parents and caregivers. If loving and peaceful people care for us, then loving and peaceful patterns will resonate with us. If those around us are sad and angry, then these disruptive patterns will feel most familiar.

We will align and be most comfortable with the energetic patterns that were imprinted in our inner matrix. Like those imprints from the womb, the imprints we receive until we are about two years of age are laid down at a foundational level in our inner matrix and become the platform for our experiences throughout the rest of our lives, unless we learn another way.

From the time we are in our mother's womb through our infancy and early childhood, our inner matrix is like a farmer's field that has been tilled and is ready for seeds to be planted. On the emotional, mental, and physical levels, our *fields* are ready for the planting of energetic patterns. But the analogy ends there. The farmer, when planting seeds in his soil, is intentional about what he sows. He carefully picks and chooses which seeds he will plant and where he will plant them. By contrast, in our earliest days, we have no ability to choose which mental, emotional, and physical patterns our first relationships will plant in the fields of our inner matrix. Whether the pattern serves us or not, every pattern we encounter in our environment is directly imprinted within us.

During our early days in these first relationships, we have no ability to reject anything we encounter in our environments. A flood of energetic information flows into our developing inner matrix, and all of these imprints make an impact. At these earliest stages, we are unable to make any choices for ourselves. We do not choose what to eat, when to be put down for sleep, what activities we will participate in, where we will go, or what experiences we will be exposed to.

We are also unable to choose the imprints and experiences from our environment. We cannot choose to keep the imprints and experiences that will create a positive effect in our lives and deny the negative imprints and experiences that will not serve us. We have no ability to reject our father's anger or our mother's shame because they will cause us to suffer. Instead, both positive and negative imprints impact us equally, and we are left at the mercy of our environments. As a result, every thought, emotion, and action we take in our lives is influenced and directed by our first relationships.

A farmer may plant thousands of seeds. Hundreds may sprout and become usable crops. Hundreds may sprout and die. Hundreds may never sprout at all, or may grow only every few years. In the same way, our mental, emotional, and physical patterns may appear to rule and define our lives. Some of these energetic imprints may appear to come and go and some seem as though they are not there at all. However, once a seed is planted in the soil, whether it sprouts or not, it will always be part of the soil. Likewise, an imprinted pattern will be part of our conditioned inner matrix, whether we are aware of the pattern or have access to it. What grows in the field is always dependent upon what was planted. A lemon seed will never become an apple tree. On the other hand, if the seed is not planted, it can never hope to flower.

Identifying the patterns that exist within our inner matrix is the first step to expanding our awareness. Taking the time to develop this increased level of awareness is critical. We cannot begin to transform a pattern within the inner matrix unless we know that it exists and is not serving what we wish to create. By expanding our awareness, we begin our journey of Conscious Transformation.

One way to expand our awareness is by reflecting on our initial experiences of life. The first relationship we experience, the relationship with our mother, has a significant bearing on every relationship to follow. In order to begin to understand our relationships with the world and others, we must first take time to reflect on what initial energetic patterns were laid down while we were in our mother's womb.

Take a few minutes and think back to when you were in the womb of your mother. What were the conditions of your mother's life? What were the experiences that were unfolding for your mother at the time you were in her womb? Did your mother have a supportive environment as she was bringing you into the world? What challenges did your mother face at this time in her life? Take time to reflect on your mother's mental, emotional, physical, and spiritual capacity at the time you were in her womb and what information would have been passed on to you that created the foundation for your inner matrix. Sit quietly and allow what is there from your inner matrix to surface from within before reading further.

If your physical birth mother is not known to you, imagine what she may have been like, what her experience might have been, and what imprints could have been passed on to you. Oftentimes, when people open themselves to an intuitive *guess* regarding their mothers' patterns, they tend to have more insight than they might imagine. That is because at some level, our mother's energetic *seeds* have already been sown, and those same patterns exist inside of us.

Also take time to reflect on who your primary caregivers were while you were a small child. What mental, emotional, physical, and spiritual capacities did these individuals have at that time to pass on to you? What were the conditions of the environment you grew up in? What imprints, both positive and negative, could have been established in your inner matrix at this time in your development? Sit quietly and allow what is there from your inner matrix to surface from within before reading further.

Through this process of asking our inner selves to reveal what has been hidden, we begin to develop conscious awareness of our imprinted patterning. This exercise is critical, given that we cannot change a pattern if we are not aware of its existence. As with all things in life, we get out of these practices what we put into them. The more time and attention we focus on these practices, the more the inner matrix will reveal to us. The greater our awareness of what information was imprinted into the inner matrix at these critical times, the more we will come to know ourselves and be able to see how we are affecting our world.

Because almost everyone has imprinted patterning that is not serving their highest good, taking time to develop this awareness is a critical step toward evolving our lives into a healthier existence. By reflecting in this way, we begin our journey into the self and take the first step toward getting to know our inner terrain. Like any exploration into uncharted territory, we are likely to find something we didn't expect. As a result, a good sense of humor about ourselves and a genuine sense of curiosity and adventure are critical components to a successful inward journey. Keep in mind that this inward journey is the greatest adventure of any lifetime.

CHAPTER 2

The Illusion of Choice

Reality leaves a lot to the imagination.

—ATTRIBUTED TO JOHN LENNON

Our state of consciousness drives the choices we make in life, but the choices we make are without awareness. What might look like choice or decision is actually predetermined by the information we received from the energetic imprinting in our first few years of life. Because our field of consciousness was planted with the seeds and patterns from our mother and early caregivers, when we make a *choice,* what we are really doing is running these imprinted patterns that someone else provided to us. Our *choices* are predetermined by the information imprinted in our inner matrix. As a result, our choices really aren't ours at all. So it could be said that the choices we make for ourselves about what we think, how we feel, and the actions we take in our lives are unconscious choices.

Until we are able to become aware of these imprints and change them, we are incapable of making choices and decisions that will take us where we want to go in life and create the realities we desire for ourselves. When we begin to make choices and decisions in our lives *with awareness,* we begin to live consciously. Now we can decide what is the best thing for our well-being instead of letting the information from our energetic imprints unknowingly direct our lives. When these energetic imprints drive us without our knowing it, this is unconscious living.

As we move from infancy into childhood, our developing language and motor skills begin to allow us to influence our environments. It may appear as though we are able to make choices with awareness at this point in our development, but this perception is not accurate. As young children, we are merely accessing patterns that were imprinted in the womb or during early childhood and then repeating those patterns.

What looks like choice is actually reaction, based upon initial programming and patterning contained in the inner matrix. In other words, as children we simply mimic or recreate the environments to which we have been exposed. When life presents us with a set of circumstances, an imprinted pattern learned from our parents or caregivers is triggered. We then act upon the pattern, and others see this action as though we are making a choice. In truth, we have not chosen the pattern or the action we have taken. Instead, both were preprogrammed for us.

Those of us who have spent time with small children and infants have watched them mimic their parents' mental and emotional states as well as their physical reactions. Psychologists tell us that before a child reaches the age of five, almost all learning comes through imitation. This includes the full range of emotions from anger to joy.

When I think of this phenomenon, I recall a hike I took in Malibu with two friends and their one-year-old daughter, Heidi. On this particular hike, instead of starting at the bottom of the mountain and hiking up, we started at the top of the mountain and hiked down. On the way down the mountain, everyone was in good spirits. Heidi was a joy, hanging out in her father's backpack, intently taking in her surroundings and taking turns cooing at all of us.

The trip up the mountain at the end of the day was another matter. By this time, Heidi's parents had become tired and hungry. Irritability soon followed. Heidi responded by mimicking their emotional states. She became irritable and fussed all the way up the hill. She could not be consoled. Once we got off of the mountain and sat down to relax for dinner at a nice restaurant, it was like flipping a switch for Heidi. As her parents relaxed, so did she. It was clear that Heidi was merely mimicking the patterns her parents were experiencing.

At one point during dinner, a funny topic came up and we all laughed. A few moments later, Heidi too began to laugh, again mimicking the social behavior even though she was not of an age where she could talk or communicate—and therefore, had no idea why we were laughing. Heidi's father even chuckled at Heidi's laughter. He looked at Heidi and said, "You have no idea why we are laughing, do you? You are just laughing because we are, aren't you?" He was amused by her automatic reaction.

Even when children move past the stage of merely mimicking their current environments, they are still not making choices with awareness. A child's primal instinct is to avoid pain and move toward pleasure. As human beings, we were wired to seek pleasure, because pleasure, in most cases, is connected to thriving, while pain is connected to danger. As a result, our so-called choice in any given situation is merely an emotional reaction to a situation perceived as painful or pleasurable. In truth, no intellectual analysis is involved at all.

When a child experiences pain or pleasure, the child's intellect rationalizes a response to support a reaction that avoids a painful situation or embraces a pleasurable one. If it feels good, a child comes up with a reason to do it. If a situation triggers a painful emotional expression, the child will find an excuse to avoid it. The emotions children experience depend on the patterns they received from their parents or caregivers. In other words, the decisions children make are not based on an intellectual analysis of what will serve them in the long run. Instead, children replay or *run* foundational patterns they received from their parents and early caregivers in reaction to emotion. As a result of those patterns, the emotion is experienced as either painful or pleasurable. A child then makes a so-called *decision* to rationalize moving toward what is pleasurable or avoiding what hurts. Many parents call this "choice."

For years at my martial-arts *dojang*, I taught a class of fifteen children, ages four to eight, and had the opportunity to see this patterning in action with children who were much older than Heidi. Frequently, parents brought in their children to try out one of our martial-arts classes. In the class, children reacted in different ways, ranging from enjoying themselves to thinking the class was boring to clinging to their parents to running out of the class or even throwing a fit. The children's reactions and whether they had painful or pleasurable experiences were functions of the patterning that existed in their inner matrix.

No matter what experience the child had during the class, upon completion of the class, the parents would routinely ask the child if he or she liked the class and would like to continue the training. The premise was that the child would then make a choice. If the child had a pleasant experience in class, he or she wanted to return for more classes. If the child had an unpleasant experience, he or she did not want to return. Because children cannot weigh their long-term best interests against their short-term discomfort and come to what would be a reasonable conclusion that such a class would ultimately serve their best interests, it makes no sense for a parent to give such a "choice" to a child who cannot developmentally exercise choice.

In these situations, it would appear as though the child was making a choice about whether he or she wished to attend future classes, but that was not actually the case. Instead, the child was having an emotional reaction to the stimulus trigger of the class environment. Two children in the same class would often have very diverse experiences based upon their individual inner matrix, and therefore their apparent choices would be different.

If, as children, we learn to make choices and decisions based upon pleasurable or painful feelings, then as we grow into adulthood, we will continue to make choices and decisions based upon pain or pleasure, because that will be all that we know. Imagine that our parents took us to the dojang and we had an unpleasant experience. After class, we then would tell our parents that we did not wish to return. Our parents would then react to our request in some way that would be defined by their own beliefs and values within their inner matrix.

If our parents allowed us not to come back, out of sympathy even though they knew the training would benefit us, we would be impacted by this situation with a flood of energetic patterns at the mental, emotional, and physical levels that would enter our inner matrix. In this instance, we would have been allowed to make a choice or decision that would alleviate our short-term discomfort at the cost of never receiving the benefit that the martial-arts training would have provided us. If our parents reinforced this same pattern time and time again, then when we became adults we would continue to act out this pattern at other "decision-making" points in our lives.

As an adult, the pattern of making choices to alleviate short-term discomfort could look like quitting a job when we encounter conflict that creates internal pain. This pattern might cause us to get divorced because our partner is no longer making us happy. It could result in our quitting a diet or exercise plan that becomes challenging to execute.

If, out of love for us, our parents decided instead that we would continue at the dojang, because they knew that the training would serve us over the long term, then our inner matrix would be imprinted with a pattern that incorporates long-term benefit into decision-making. This situation would also create a flood of energetic patterns at the mental, emotional, and physical levels that would enter our inner matrix. If our parents reinforced this same pattern over time, when we became adults, we would continue to act out this long-term–oriented pattern of delaying gratification to achieve a desired goal.

With a long-term orientation, when our jobs and relationships became painful, we would be able to consider the long-term implications of leaving those situations and would have the capacity to make decisions based on more than pain and pleasure. In this case, we would have been taught as children that pain-versus-pleasure is only one factor to be considered in our decision-making, and we would carry that pattern into adulthood. When our relationships became difficult, we might look for long-term solutions that would benefit the relationships over time. When our jobs became challenging and we experienced internal strife, we might first attempt to improve our performance and resolve personal conflict, thereby bettering our long-term financial prospects. Despite short-term discomfort experienced during a diet or exercise plan, we would be more likely to stay with our program long enough to experience the benefits the program has in store for us.

On the other hand, if our parents told us to continue at the dojang and we came to hate the practice and resented having to go over time, we would have a different pattern altogether. If this pattern were reinforced time and time again, our inner matrix would be trained not to allow pain to influence our decision-making. This pattern would be carried throughout our adulthood as well.

When we encountered a dead-end job that was taking us nowhere, we would not leave to look for something better. When we found ourselves in a relationship that did not serve us, we would stay despite the pain we were experiencing. We might never begin a diet or exercise program that could have the potential to better our lives.

When we are children, our parents make decisions for us, and through this process, they train our inner matrix how to engage in decision-making. When we move into puberty and our teenage years, we have the ability to make decisions for ourselves for the first time. It is at this stage that we begin to establish our own independence.

However, during this time, our emotions are often high and extremely erratic, fueled in part by fluctuating hormone levels. The ability to step out of emotional patterning and into intellectual reasoning becomes increasingly important. Most foundational patterns have been established and anchored by the time we become teenagers. If we lack the ability to step out of the emotional patterning and into rational thinking, those same emotional patterns with their mental justifications begin to be repeated over and over again throughout our teenage years.

In the teenage years, we establish mental and emotional patterning on an even deeper physiological level. We can picture how these patterns are established in the neuro-circuitry of our brain by visualizing a mountainside covered with fresh powder that has not yet been skied upon. When we have an experience in life that triggers a mental, emotional, or physical reaction, it is like a skier going down the side of that mountain and creating a path or rut in the snow. If the skier skis that same path over and over again, a deep rut is made in the snow. As the rut becomes deeper, the skier is able to travel that same path with greater ease and at faster speeds as he or she becomes more practiced skiing the rut. However, creating a new path is difficult as the skier becomes stuck in the deep rut they have established. At some point, the rut becomes so deep that the skier cannot even see beyond its high walls, let alone hope to climb out.

When we reinforce the same mental, emotional, and physical patterns, a strong neuropathway is created in the brain. The more this neuropathway is reinforced, the harder it is to change and the stronger it becomes. The patterns produced in the neuropathway are active every moment of our lives, creating for us the same experiences again and again. As a result, our jobs, homes, relationships, and other external situations may change, but our experiences in these situations remain the same.

Even when our running the neuropathway causes us to suffer and fail, we are unable to choose something different because, neurologically we have no other pathway available to us. In order to go a different way, we have to create a new path. However, most of us do not know how to consciously create new neuropathways in the brain so that we can make new experiences possible. Because these new ways of being are unknown to us, we cannot even see what might be possible beyond our current patterns. Our patterns become *totalizing*: they completely define our experiences.

To demonstrate the intense power our patterns have over our perceptions, at my programs, I often have all of the participants focus on an orchid and then share what thoughts, feelings, and memories come up for them. The wide variety of different responses that are shared is surprising to the participants. Although all of the participants are looking at the same flower, the range of experiences from one person to the next is vast and unpredictable, as a result of their own individualized patterning. Reactions to the flower range from an individual experiencing anger over an old girlfriend whose favorite flower happened to be an orchid to a person experiencing peace and happiness as the flower made him think of his vacation in Hawaii. Yet another participant experienced deep grief and sorrow, even being brought to tears, as she thought of the orchids at her grandmother's funeral, only to be followed moments later with joy and elation remembering herself as a little girl playing in the flowerbed at that same grandmother's house.

The truth is, at the end of the day, the orchid is just a flower sitting in a vase. Those are the facts. The experience each person has in relationship to the orchid has nothing to do with the flower itself. The orchid is simply acting as a trigger that stimulates the internal patterns that already exist within each person. As participants focus on the flower, they each experience their own mental, emotional, and physical patterns as their neuropathways are stimulated. Despite the fact that no one is in Hawaii or at their grandmother's house, the response elicited by that little flower is a very intense experience that feels quite real to those who are participating in the exercise.

I use this practice to show people how our internal patterns create our experiences in every given moment. The responses that people have are always so diverse that it becomes clear that experience is not caused by what *shows up* in the present environment outside of us, but is instead a function of what we carry *inside*. I also use this example to show how unrelated events and life experiences become connected to one another and make past experiences our present reality.

Another example of the power of our internal patterns can usually be found by reflecting back on the first romantic relationship from our teenage years. In the beginning of the relationship, we felt as though we were in love. We were liberated, excited, ecstatic, and fulfilled. We felt as though life could not possible get any better. These emotional experiences lasted a week, a month, or for some of us, even years. In many cases, our highly pleasurable experiences in this first romantic relationship were followed by extremely painful encounters.

Perhaps we were in love with our boyfriend or girlfriend and thought nothing could go wrong. Then we found out that our significant other decided he or she didn't love us anymore. Sometimes this revelation was coupled with learning that our partner wished to be with someone else. Sometimes our loved one simply moved away and did not want to have a long-distance relationship. With such experiences came a range of emotions, including anger, betrayal, unworthiness, disappointment, grief, and sadness. In those moments in our young lives, we often believed that life could not get any worse.

After the relationship ended, the experience was not over from an emotional standpoint. Sometimes, these intense emotions lasted a week, a month, or even years. After the initial emotional onslaught, we found ourselves reflecting back on the situation over and over again. We remembered the good times, the happy moments, and this stimulated the same highly pleasurable emotions we knew in the relationship as if they were happening in the present. We also remembered the not-so-good times in the relationship, and in some cases, the traumatic endings. These reflections triggered in the present the same painful emotions we felt in the past during bad times in the relationship.

As a result, we experienced these memories of the past as though they were happening all over again. This phenomenon occurs because the internal experience that surfaces for us inside is exactly the same whether we think of a situation from our past, something occurring in the moment, or a possible reality that could be our future. Although our actual relationship might have been over for weeks, months, or years, our inner experiences are kept alive from a neurological standpoint by these times of reflection, because, internally, the mental, emotional, and physical sensations are the same as the original experience.

In some cases, the experience of remembered events becomes even stronger than the original occurrences. As we reflect over and over again, we dig the ruts in our brains deeper and deeper and cement the connections inherent in that experience. In our example of a first romantic relationship, the connection formed was between love and pain, two concepts that should not be wired together but often are. The reflective process keeps these internal imprints and patterns active. As a result, in order to experience love, we must also experience pain—because these internal expressions have been connected into one intricate pattern through life experience.

Even though these patterns may be painful and we desire to alleviate that pain, the pattern is all we have access to, so it is not possible to create another experience. The pattern becomes familiar, and as human beings, we feel comfortable with the familiar. As a result, we press the *repeat* button and play the same sad song over and over again. These patterns become our default programs, and these connections between various emotions play out time and time again in our lives. Our experience in life has taught us that love will hurt, and because we have no other internal pattern to play, it will.

In order to understand how emotions become interconnected in our energetic patterns, it is helpful to look at specific brain components called neurons. In neurology, scientists speak of neurons as the building blocks of the nervous system. Neurons are connections in the brain that are responsible for communicating sensory information throughout the brain by way of energetic pulses. Every time we experience a thought, emotion, or physical sensation, neurons corresponding to that experience fire an electrical pulse within the brain.

Neurologists, who study the brain, have a common phrase: "Neurons that fire together, wire together." Because of the way the brain has been wired through experience, the firing of one neuron triggers the firing of connected neurons, and so on and so forth to form an intricate pattern. In other words, if you experience certain thoughts, emotions, and physical sensations together, over time, they will become connected and will automatically fire together.

In our example above, if we experience a highly pleasurable state such as falling in love, and this is immediately followed by an extremely unpleasant experience such as betrayal, as far as the brain is concerned, love and betrayal are now connected. Unless interrupted, these neuronal patterns will automatically continue to fire together, stimulating the same pleasing or displeasing dynamic over and over again, long after the initial experience has ended. Even though reason tells us that love does not have to come to a painful end, our brain has connected the two and we will react accordingly. Because the two emotional states are physically wired together, the brain cannot ignore the connection. Therefore, when one is triggered, the other will fire as well, creating our internal experience of life at a mental, emotional, and physical level and programming our inner matrix.

This phenomenon is known as *conditioned response*. Conditioned response has long been recognized in psychology. A scientist by the name of Ivan Pavlov was awarded the Nobel Prize in 1904 in Physiology and Medicine for a famous study he conducted that illustrated this type of conditioned response. In a series of laboratory experiments, Dr. Pavlov rang a bell immediately before he fed a group of dogs. As a result, the dogs began to connect the sound of the bell with food and, therefore, in anticipation of being fed, the dogs began to salivate when the bell rang.

Early on in his study, Dr. Pavlov would ring a bell, the dogs would salivate, and then Dr. Pavlov would feed the dogs. Later in the study, Dr. Pavlov began ringing the bell without feeding the dogs. The dogs automatically responded to the bell over and over again by salivating, even though there was no food. As far as the dogs' brains were concerned, the sound of a bell equated to food, and the fact that no food showed up in their environment did not alter their response.

Even over time, when the dogs' environment no longer included food, when the bell sounded, the dogs' brains continued to connect the two because there was a hardwired neurological pairing between the bell and food. The fact that food was not actually appearing did not modify the dogs' response, because there was no intellectual analysis taking place, only conditioned reaction. The dogs had no other pattern to run but this one; that was how their brains had been wired through experience. The connection between the bell and food had been made and therefore, no matter what showed up in their environment, once the bell rang, the dogs salivated. This is conditioned response.

The human brain works the same way. Once neurons are wired together, they will automatically fire together without the person first considering the actual facts of a situation. For example, in the above scenario where love has resulted in a painful experience, as adults, a new romance may show up in our lives, and we may feel angry and sad, even though that person has done nothing that would logically cause such a response. We may be jealous and suspicious of our new partner, despite his or her actual devotion to us. As a result, the relationship will suffer.

We take this action despite the fact that we care about our relationship and would not intentionally set out to destroy the relationship or hurt the person we love. With a conditioned response, there is simply no conscious choice involved and no awareness of what we are doing, why we are doing it, or the impact it will have on our relationship. Our action is merely a conditioned pattern that exists inside of us, and we have no access to other ways of being.

* * *

A real-life example of how these patterns play out in our relationships can be seen through Kirk, a regular attendee at my workshops. From my discussions with him, I deduced that Kirk was born to a mother who believed that Kirk was born for her. When we think of a mother, we think of unconditional love. Ideally, a mother gives love freely to her child and believes that she is to be there for her child. In Kirk's situation, I perceived the opposite was true and that Kirk's mother believed that Kirk was there to do something for her. When Kirk's mother would do things for her son, she would tell him what a sacrifice she was making for him. She made it clear that her son owed her and was obligated to pay her back for everything she did.

The imprints Kirk's mother received in childhood established core patterns of shame, anger, resentment, and guilt in her inner matrix, which she experienced and identified as love. We can come to understand how these patterns were established in her if we look at her early childhood memories. Her parents were alcoholics who put their needs before hers. She remembers trying to stay out of the way while her parents argued and drank. She went without basic things that she needed, because her parents spent their money on alcohol instead of taking care of her.

As a result, Kirk's mother came to believe that she had to support her parents' needs and that her own needs were not important. As a child, she deeply desired to be nurtured and loved but had no one who had the capacity or patterning of love or nurturing to offer her. Because she only knew shame, anger, resentment, guilt, and the desire to be loved, those were the only patterns and energetic imprints she could pass onto Kirk. These patterns were imprinted upon Kirk starting when he was in his mother's womb and were reinforced throughout his life and well into adulthood.

When Kirk was born, his mother still carried the deep desire to be nurtured and loved by her parents that had gone unfulfilled, creating and establishing the pattern of abandonment in her inner matrix. She came to look to her son to fulfill the desire she carried deep within her to be nurtured and loved by her parents. Kirk, being his mother's son, could not possibly give his mother the love of a parent—not only was he just a child and not responsible for or capable of parenting, but no one had imprinted Kirk with the ability to love in the first place.

Whenever Kirk failed to meet his mother's expectations of loving and nurturing her, the patterns she carried of abandonment, resentment, shame, guilt, and anger that existed in her inner matrix were triggered. As a result, she believed her son was responsible for making her feel abandoned, resentful, shameful, guilty, and angry. In truth, these patterns existed in her long before Kirk was born. Kirk's mother could not see that Kirk was not responsible for these patterns, because she was not aware of the patterns she had been imprinted with from her own parents. She only knew that she experienced these patterns when Kirk failed to meet her expectations. So, she attributed responsibility for these feelings to Kirk, as if he were the cause of them. This resulted in Kirk's mother believing that her son, Kirk, owed her a debt and was obligated to pay her back any time she did anything for him. She believed he had failed to adequately appreciate her and sufficiently reciprocate for the sacrifices she felt she regularly made for him.

As Kirk matured, he experienced shame, anger, resentment, and guilt whenever his mother did anything for him. Eventually, the mere sound of her voice or the sight of her name on his caller ID could cause rage to rise up in him. Kirk was confused by his reaction to his mother. He could not understand why he was so angry when his mother would do a seemingly kind act for him, such as making dinner for his family, helping with household chores, or babysitting his children.

Kirk told himself that his mother loved him and that he should be grateful instead of angry at her. Kirk could see that his reaction did not line up as a normal response to someone giving to him and doing things for him. As a result, Kirk felt that there was something inherently wrong with him, because he did not feel gratitude and love for his mother. Instead, he felt shame and guilt for the anger and resentment he carried regarding her, when she appeared to be doing so much for him.

As an adult, Kirk found himself in relationships where he did not experience love, even in his marriage, when his wife deeply loved him. When his wife did things for him, instead of feeling love and gratitude, Kirk felt anger. Kirk believed that his wife was doing kind things for him, such as making dinner, doing the laundry, or offering affection or nurturing, so that she could keep score and hold those acts of kindness over his head, with an expectation that he pay her back. Kirk then found himself doing things for his wife out of a sense of obligation and duty, breeding further resentment toward his wife. Kirk was unable to experience his wife's genuine love for him.

For many years, Kirk was miserable and deeply desired a change in his relationship with his wife. However, nothing he tried could change the pattern of guilt, shame, anger, and resentment he experienced in his marriage. As a result, Kirk's relationship crumbled and came to the brink of divorce. If Kirk had not discovered the work of Conscious Transformation and acquired the ability to access new experiences and ways of being outside of his inherited patterns, his destiny would have been divorce, and his family would have broken apart. Even if he had paid the high price of divorce, Kirk still would only have had access to the patterns of guilt, shame, anger, and resentment within him. He would have had no other choice except to recreate this experience in his next relationship.

The reason that Kirk could not experience his wife's love was that Kirk only had access to the patterns that were imprinted within him as a child and reinforced throughout his life. The pattern of unconditional love was not a pattern Kirk had access to, making it impossible for him to experience it. Instead, he saw and experienced life through the patterns of guilt, shame, anger, and resentment that defined all his experiences. No matter what his wife did, Kirk's experience was the same. Therefore, it was impossible for him to create and experience the loving relationship he desired.

If we were able to speak to Kirk's grandmother about her childhood and life, we would find the same patterns and imprints of experience and the same unfulfilled desires. So, as you can see from this story, imprints of patterns are passed from one generation to the next, with the inability to create a different experience or reality. Even if there is a desire for a different experience in life, without the proper internal training, it is impossible.

Kirk is a prime example of the legacy and power of our first relationships and their impact on all of the relationships that follow. The good news is that through the practices presented in this book, we can learn the tools necessary to break the bonds of habitual patterns and shift the destiny of our lives and the legacy we leave to our children.

As you can see, the imprints and patterns that we received from others become the entire range of our life experience. We are not capable of experiencing anything outside of these unconscious patterns. As adults, we begin to see life through the lenses or filters of our narrow range of expressions. Over time, we come to believe that this is who we are and what life is.

Most of us exist in a place of habit, simply reacting in a consistent way to the stimulus of our environments, triggering the same unseen core-patterning, resulting in the same life experiences we've always known. Unless we learn tools that empower us to shift and change our inner matrix, we will repeat the same set of limited experiences for the rest of our lives. The way we think, feel, and sense our world creates our perception of the world, which in turn molds our external life. In other words, ultimately, our inner workings create our outer experiences.

From conception through adulthood, if we do not develop the skills to consciously evolve ourselves, we automatically become a product of our early environment. We become trapped in a prison of our unconscious patterns, unable to make conscious choices. Unaware that this dynamic is at work, we try repeatedly to change our lives but find ourselves having the same experiences over and over again, eliciting the same results. Instead of having real choice in our life, we only have the illusion of choice. The longer we live in our habitual reactions, the harder it is to shift and change our patterns so that we can step into the life we desire. The good news is that no matter our age, if we are given the tools to elevate our consciousness, even old dogs can step out of conditioned response and into new ways of being.

CHAPTER 3

The Mind's Cage

You can't solve a problem from the same consciousness
that created it. You must learn to see the world anew.

—ALBERT EINSTEIN

Old patterns imprinted during our early relationships lie in our mental, emotional, and physical bodies. The mind can serve as a bridge or tool for unlocking these patterns in each of the aspects of the inner matrix. In order to unlock that door and taste freedom, we must understand the mind and gain the capacity to *think the mind* instead of allowing the *mind to think us*. In other words, we must train the mind like an athlete trains the body for a race.

We start with the mind because of our ability to immediately access and direct its conscious aspects. The mind, like the heart, is always operating and fulfilling its purpose. The heart's purpose is to constantly pump blood, carrying oxygen and nutrients throughout the body via the circulatory system; it does so without our awareness of this happening, without ceasing. The mind's purpose is to think. It is constantly creating thoughts, beliefs, and concepts, giving us the ability to function in life and interact with our environments. If the mind were to stop serving its purpose, we would slip into a vegetative state, unable to function. The mind is constantly thinking, even when we are not aware of thinking itself.

The heart is always beating, even if we are not aware of its beating. If you are a trained athlete, you may check your pulse rate every day while exercising, which may give you an awareness of how fast your heart is beating. However, you cannot change the heart's way of functioning. You cannot stop and start your heart beating, make it beat erratically, or alter the way the blood flows.

In contrast, we can change the mind's way of functioning. We can *think* the mind instead of the mind thinking us. Anyone, at any time, can immediately access and direct the mind as they choose. If you were asked to think a positive or constructive thought about yourself, you would immediately be able to think several such thoughts. If you were asked to think something negative or critical about yourself, you could direct your mind to think those thoughts within a moment. You might not believe the thoughts you were thinking about yourself, but you could still think those thoughts any time, at will.

However, most people do not have the proper training to direct their minds consistently. Cognitive scientists have determined that as a rule of thumb we are unaware of what we are thinking 95 percent of the time, let alone directing our thoughts. With training, we can alter the condition of our minds by stopping its constant mental chatter, changing the caliber of our thoughts and establishing new ways of thinking that have previously not been known to us.

The immediate access we have to shifting and changing our mental patterns is not the same for our emotional, physical, and intuitive patterns. For example, we can all think of a time when we have been very angry. In such a state, we cannot immediately just *decide* to become peaceful in an instant. The same would be true if we are in a place of peace and serenity. We could not step into feeling rage at a moment's notice. Although it is possible to gain the capacity to influence our emotions instantaneously and at will, this skill is only available to us after we have properly trained and developed the mind.

A good example of how the untrained mind affects other aspects of our lives can be found by taking a look at the typical New Year's resolutions to *get in shape*. Workout facilities are filled to capacity during the month of January. By February or March, the numbers have significantly dwindled. The reason for the drop in attendance is not because people cannot physically handle the exercise. Instead, it is because they have weak minds and lack the mental discipline to successfully complete their New Year's resolutions.

If we haven't been to the gym for a while, the morning after a hard workout can be anything but pleasurable. As a result, if we do not have a disciplined mind, like those children at the dojang, we quit in response to the pain we experience. In such a situation, we are reacting to emotion and patterning instead of making a conscious choice to proceed with something that would clearly be healthy and beneficial for us. In this example, our minds are weak, so our bodies stay weak as well.

Most of us live our lives in an unconscious state, unaware of our thoughts, the effect those thoughts have on us, and how the thoughts are directing and creating our lives. As we learn to become mindful of what we are thinking, we step into a place of awareness, moving out of unconscious thinking. That is, we evolve beyond the state where our minds are *thinking* us. This space of awareness gives us the ability to actually *choose* our thoughts. Conscious thinking is the ability to choose what thoughts our minds will create, with an awareness of the effect those thoughts will have on us. Through conscious choice, we shift our current mental state and begin the journey of Conscious Transformation within ourselves. Learning to consciously evolve gives us access to making our dreams a reality. Without the ability to shift internal patterns, the mind is a cage. My Kabbalistic rabbi also likened the mind to a prisoner, caged within itself, an idea based upon Plato's "Allegory of the Cave."

Imagine you were born in a prison cell. This cell is all you have known your entire life. Food and water are brought to you in your cell, as is everything else that is necessary to survive. Because this cell is all you have ever known, you have no awareness of the larger prison confines beyond your cell's walls. You don't even realize that the walls are confining you. One day, you awake from your sleep and notice something is different: a door that you did not even know existed in the wall of your prison is now open.

At first, you feel strange and awkward, because something has changed. After a while, curiosity fills you and you begin to peer through the cell door. For the first time, you see a hallway and hundreds of other cells just like yours. At first, you do not dare to step through the open door. You are gripped by fear. Instead of venturing out, you stay in the familiar safety of your cell. As time passes, food and water cease to arrive in your cell, and you experience the intolerable pain of thirst and hunger, which increases your yearning to venture outside. Finally, when the discomfort becomes too great, you step out into the unknown and begin to explore the inside of the greater prison.

Time and time again, this experience repeats itself, and you venture farther and farther out. Eventually, you discover a door leading outside the prison, and one day, you step through it and begin to wander the prison grounds. Next, you go through the prison gate, stepping outside the prison grounds and into the nearby town. Finally, you step foot outside of the town and begin to explore the vast world that is available to you. You wander the beaches, the mountains, and the forests. You discover cities and ancient ruins. You sail the seas to faraway lands. This new world is so vast. You see that it is impossible to know all the nooks and crannies of your new home as you once did your prison cell.

Over time, you gain awareness that this world is ever-changing and that nothing remains the same for long. As time passes, you learn to build houses, bridges, and roads. You learn to find your own food. One day you realize that there is no longer a yearning inside of you for anything. You become aware that you were actually the architect of the prison that once held you. For the first time, you know that you are truly free of its confines.

Although you are continuously expanding in this new world, something draws you back to the prison from which you escaped. It is compassion for the inmates who are still imprisoned and unaware of the world outside of their confinement. Seeing your former self in the current prison inmates, you return to the prison out of a sense of love and a desire that everyone know the freedom you experience in the world outside of the prison.

Many of us can relate to the example of being trapped in the prison of our own thoughts, emotions, and sensations. While we are confined, we face the same thoughts, emotions, and experiences day in and day out. Oftentimes, we know that something is missing, but having not experienced anything else, we are reluctant to take that first step. However, once we do step over the threshold of our cell and begin to shift out of our current ways of thinking, feeling, and acting, we open ourselves to new possibilities of experience within us. As we sensed, these new potential experiences always existed, but we were not aware of them and did not have access to them. Within this space lives an array of new ways of thinking, feeling, and taking action that are suddenly available.

Through the practice of Conscious Transformation, we free the mind, expand our emotional range, empower the body, and gain access to our hidden inner potential. New thoughts, emotions, and strengths develop within us and open a new internal world that reshapes our external existence as well. As in the prison story, we only have access to what we know, and we cannot envision what lies beyond our current state of being, because we have not yet experienced it. Like the prisoner in his cell, we are unaware of the vast world beyond.

The only way to know our internal world is to step beyond our cell. Anything we imagine while we are in our cell is just an extrapolation of the cell itself. It is just an extension of what we already know and have experienced. While caged, our imagination cannot begin to approximate the majesty of existence beyond our four walls. Once we open to new ways of being, then we have access on a whole new level and our existence shifts, changes, and expands. Over time, even this new, more expansive state becomes stagnant, and we repeat this stepping out, over and over again, as we move forward into new eras both internally and externally.

The way to escape from a prison is to understand how it operates, where the doors are, and how to open those doors. So, the first step to freeing ourselves from our minds is to understand what our minds are and how they operate. This will give us the keys to unlocking the doors that confine us, giving us access to greater awareness. Before I offer some of my foundational practices for Conscious Transformation, let's explore some additional context regarding the mind and how it operates.

The mind is a pure space or void, containing the energy and power to manifest any vibration that is placed in that space. Every thought is a vibration of energy. Each thought exists along either a spectrum of divine love or a spectrum of fear. In any given moment, the mind is either operating and aligning with the aspect of divine love or the aspect of fear, but never both of these. It is simply impossible for the mind to be in a state of divine love and fear at the same time. In any given moment, there is a choice to be made.

Divine love is an experience of expansion. When the mind is thinking positive and constructive thoughts, the mind is in a state of expansion. When we think about the opportunities and possibilities in our lives and all that is going well for us, the mind is expanding. When we focus on our good qualities and our strengths, we expand as well. When we think about the people we love and all of their wonderful characteristics, our minds are aligned with divine love.

Fear, on the other hand, is an experience of contraction. When the mind is thinking negatively, the mind is in a state of contraction. When we think thoughts about the uncertainties of our lives and all of our perceived problems, the mind is contracting. When we focus on what is wrong with us and all of our weaknesses, we contract as well. When we think of our spouse or partner's shortcomings, our minds are aligned with fear.

As we grew up, our minds were imprinted with patterns of thought. Many of these patterns are interwoven with fearful, contracting thoughts, beliefs, and concepts that we inherited from our parents and environments. When the mind is left unsupervised, it often plays the tapes of those negative patterns, aligning us with fear. These patterns of thought place us in a state of contraction that significantly shapes our lives. As the mind plays these patterns over and over, it activates and reinforces these fearful aspects, ultimately creating suffering and chaos. The key to eliminating suffering and unlocking higher states of consciousness begins in our minds.

When we consciously direct our thoughts, on the other hand, we can align our minds with the high vibration of divine love and expansion. As we create new thoughts in this alignment, we can establish new patterns of thinking that will benefit us. The more frequently we direct our minds and align with higher vibrations, the more expansion we welcome into our lives. Through this process, we set the foundation for manifesting a new reality aligned with love instead of fear. Through this process, we can alleviate our suffering and intentionally construct a new way of being. This way of being in the world aligns us with our vision for an extraordinary life.

* * *

Our minds are laid down in three layers: conscious, subconscious, and unconscious. For the purposes of our work here, I have developed a model for each of the layers to give us a blueprint for working with our minds. In this model, *thoughts* occur on the conscious level, *beliefs* on the subconscious level, and *core concepts* on the unconscious level of our minds.

The first layer, our conscious mind, is the aspect that we can easily be aware of as we go about our day-to-day lives. The thoughts we are aware of exist in the conscious mind. Anytime we wish to tune into our thoughts, we can. As we have discussed, for most of us, the conscious mind runs on autopilot. As the untrained mind creates chaos, the trained and conscious mind provides us with the ability to make choices and exercise judgment. We can use our conscious mind to assess information in our environment and determine which paths serve us and which paths do not. A trained and conscious mind provides discernment that allows us to create the states of being we desire.

When we are accessing our minds at the level of thought, we are working with our conscious minds. However, because the mind is laid down in layers, when we are engaging thought, it is like touching the surface of the ocean. If we wish to change the mind's composition, we must dive underneath our thoughts to discover the foundational beliefs and concepts that are creating our thoughts and holding them in place.

The subconscious is the level of the mind that lies just below the conscious mind. The subconscious mind is the realm of our beliefs.

Beliefs support and even establish our thoughts. Although we may be aware of some of our beliefs, there are many more that are hidden from our awareness in portions of our subconscious to which we have no access. The subconscious mind serves as the bridge between the conscious and unconscious minds. It creates rules and guidelines to build our frames of reference and directs how our conscious minds function. As a result, it is critical that we begin to examine what beliefs support the thoughts that we are having and uncover those parts of the subconscious mind that are hiding.

Belief structures, like thoughts, are aligned with either love or fear. If we have a belief that is aligned with fear, it will create many thoughts that are aligned with fear. If a belief is aligned with divine love, then the thoughts it supports will be of the same vibration. If I believe that *I can achieve whatever I set my mind to,* this belief will support and create thoughts such as *I am capable; life is exciting; I will be successful; I am unstoppable; I am smart;* and *I can overcome anything.* On the other hand, if I believe that *I can't do anything right,* this belief will support and create thoughts such as I *can't do it; why try; things never work out for me; I'm never going to succeed at anything, life is so hard; I am stupid;* and *everyone is against me.*

When we begin to identify the beliefs that are operating in the subconscious mind and creating our thought patterns, we can reflect on which beliefs are serving us and which are not. If not, we can shift and change those beliefs to reflect a state with which we wish to align. Shifting and changing our beliefs will cause a much more extensive and lasting impact than merely changing our thoughts. The reason for this is that our beliefs serve as the *structure supporting our thoughts.*

As we saw in the above model, one belief can support a multitude of thought patterns. Even if we are consciously aware that such thoughts are potentially destructive and we shift and change the thoughts as they arise, our underlying belief will continue to fuel the creation of more thoughts aligned with the destructive pattern. If we shift the belief that is creating such thoughts, then the thoughts will shift.

Therefore, the impact is exponentially greater when we change and shift our beliefs.

The unconscious is the deepest and most powerful level of our minds. All of our experiences, from the moment of conception to the moment we transition from our human bodies, are recorded in the unconscious, even when we do not remember them. Our pre-language experiences, along with our most emotionally intense and frequent experiences in life, form the foundational level of our unconscious. Those experiences determine our perceptions of the outside world, how we see ourselves in relationship to the outside world, and the type of relationship we have with ourselves and others.

Despite the power that this realm wields over our lives, we do not have awareness of what lies in our unconscious minds without highly specialized training. We can think of the unconscious mind as akin to the hard drive of a computer. Just as the hard drive contains computer code for the computer's operating system that is neither seen nor understood by the average user, so the unconscious mind contains the *code* for our beliefs and thoughts. For example, if you wish to run an application on a Mac computer, it has to be consistent with the operating system for the Mac. If the application is not in alignment with a Mac operating system but instead is made for a Windows PC, it will not work. The unconscious mind's method of programming is through our hidden, core concepts. The mind cannot sustain thoughts and beliefs that are out of alignment with our core concepts.

We have a very limited number of core concepts, but they silently rule and guide our lives. All of our beliefs and thoughts stem from a few basic core concepts stored in the unconscious mind. *I am loved,* and *I am unworthy* are two examples of core concepts that many individuals carry. If our core concept is that *I am unworthy*, the resulting beliefs and thoughts that will be created and supported in us will be diametrically opposed to the beliefs and thoughts that would be created based on a core concept of *I am loved.* If we do not bring our core concepts into our awareness, then we are at their mercy, unaware of how and why we are creating what shows up in our external environment. Our unconscious is the largest and most significant part of our minds and has the greatest influence in determining what shows up in our lives.

These hidden core patterns in our unconscious minds are the root cause for why we have the same experiences over and over again. If, through our early relationships, we were imprinted with joy, vibrancy, and love, we will see these patterns play over and over again throughout our adult relationships. If instead we experienced anger, grief, and shame through these first relationships, then we will see these patterns show up, despite our best efforts to create something different in our lives. This cycle can be particularly frustrating when we are not even aware that it exists. Because these cycles arise out of core patterns in our unconscious, usually we are not aware of how or why we are creating certain experiences. We just know that we are suffering.

Because these core energetic patterns live in the deepest layers of the unconscious, we have the least access to those mental patterns that have the most power over creating our lives. Learning how to see the mind and uncover what operates in its unseen portions can drive significant change in the entirety of our inner matrix. This is why positive affirmations alone take an extremely long time to create change: they only address the surface level of our minds and neglect the vastly more powerful structures that lie beneath.

It can be extremely challenging to shift the nature of our unconscious patterns, because, unlike our physical bodies, what lives in our minds is intangible. We cannot see, taste, touch, or feel our thoughts. When our bodies are sick, we may run a temperature or get a stomachache. At that point, we know that we need to take action to help heal the body. But when the mind is not doing well, it often goes untended, because we have no way of seeing the unconscious mind that is running the show.

It is critical that we begin to embark on the work of training the mind, moving from understanding our thoughts and beliefs to ultimately our core concepts. We can think of the undisciplined mind as a weed growing in our yard. What lives at the level of the unconscious is the root. If we mow down the weed, dealing only with that which we can see, the weed will quickly grow back because we have left its root. In order to embrace permanent transformation, we must go to the root of the problem to shift and change the faulty core concepts that serve as the foundation and impetus for our beliefs and thoughts. Pulling the weed out, root and all, is the path to lasting change.

Many of us are aware of the famous spiritual teachings about the importance of being fully present in each and every moment. This may sound like an easy thing to accomplish, but without training, it is extremely difficult if not impossible to execute. The untrained mind does not want to stay in the present, in the moment, where all is uncertain, but instead seeks the comfort of the past or future where the mind knows what has happened or can create its own fantasies about what will happen. The meditative practice of mindfulness that I teach focuses on learning how to stay fully present in the moment while allowing all thoughts and feelings to pass by without judgment or attachment.

Once we have developed the skill of staying fully present in the moment, we gain the ability to consciously choose our thoughts, beliefs, and concepts. This ability empowers us to define our moments and create our reality. As explained before, there are only two aspects in creation, those aligning us with divine love or those aligning us with fear. In any moment, when we consciously choose to embody patterns aligning with divine love, we activate this infinite power from within, and the momentum of that energy flows through us, influencing all aspects of our lives.

As explained above, most people have no idea what their mind looks like, since they cannot see it in the mirror. As a result, the best way to get to know what the mind is like is to spend time with it, just like you would any other relationship. In our busy world filled with distractions, most of us spend very little time just being with ourselves. To begin discovering the imprints in the mind, just sit with the mind for twenty minutes a day. During that time, do not play music, focus on your breath, meditate, or use any techniques to *try* to quiet the mind. Instead, just sit in a quiet place, close your eyes, and give the mind permission to think whatever it wishes.

Sometimes, the mind is quiet in the beginning because it does not wish to be seen. However, after a while, the mind will begin to think itself, and you will have a front-row seat for experiencing what is in your mind. At this point, a variety of experiences can surface from the mind, depending on the patterns existing within the inner matrix. Sometimes, we see how beautiful we are on the inside. Sometimes, what we see is how ugly we are on the inside. During this practice, it is not uncommon for us to become aware of how extremely chaotic and erratic our minds are. This is normal. No matter what we discover within ourselves, it is all a beneficial and positive experience. We are gaining awareness of what exists inside and stepping into the first level of Conscious Transformation.

After doing this practice for a month, a student of mine named Caroline asked me why I disliked her so much. Although she was joking, she realized that the state of her mind was no laughing matter. She had always believed that she was an optimistic, professional woman who had highly developed skills of focus and concentration. Through this practice, she learned that the stories she had created about how she thought her mind was operating were pure fantasy.

To Caroline's surprise, the majority of her thoughts were actually very negative, unfocused, and repetitive. She discovered that her mind jumped from one thought to another, often failing to even complete one thought, let alone a topic, before moving onto the next one. She found that almost daily she would return to a handful of sad or tragic memories from her past, deepening the experience of suffering inherent in those patterns. She was surprised to discover that she did not have as many different thoughts as she had believed before she began to do the practice. She came to realize that she was playing the same thought patterns in her mind over and over again, very much like putting a song on repeat.

When Caroline questioned why I had assigned this exercise, I explained that I ask students to engage in this practice because through sitting and observing their minds they come to realize, as she did, that they do not have a wide spectrum of different thoughts, beliefs, and concepts flowing through their minds. In actuality, they are playing the same few narrow patterns of thinking over and over again. These thought patterns are aligning with a certain level of vibration, creating the current outcomes in their lives.

Because the thoughts playing in our minds usually do not align with what we truly desire, we must change the patterns of thought. When we change our thought patterns, we can align our minds with the life we want to create. Various sources in popular culture have defined insanity as "doing the same thing over and over again and expecting that you will get a different result." The thought patterns playing in the mind will align us with a specific experience equal to the vibration of those thoughts. Because thoughts are placed in the power of the mind, they will manifest in our lives, at some level. Whether we know they are playing or not and whether we desire them or not, thoughts placed in the mind will create just the same. It is not until we are able to shift the mental tapes playing in our minds that we can manifest the experiences we truly desire.

Among the patterns playing in Caroline's mind were negative thoughts about herself. Caroline believed that she was unworthy of receiving love. She believed that if she loved someone, they would leave her. As a result, Caroline worried about her husband asking for a divorce and something tragic happening to one of her children. Caroline was afraid to be too close to her spouse, convinced that the relationship was only temporary and that the more vulnerable she was to her husband, the more he would hurt her in the end. She was angry at him and believed that he did not truly care about her. Caroline was often an over-protective mother who feared the worst, even in benign situations with her children. Despite the fact that Caroline had been very financially successful, she worried incessantly about money, believing that she did not deserve the money she made. As a result, she was unable to enjoy her successes. She believed that it would all soon come to an end.

Once Caroline was able to see her thought patterns, she saw the connection between these patterns and what was showing up in her life.

She realized that her husband actually was committed and that her fears were just an illusion. Caroline realized that as a result of her negative thoughts about him, she was keeping herself distant from him. In their relationship, this distancing sometimes showed up as conflict; other times, it looked like Caroline was avoiding being alone with her husband.

Because Caroline was so angry with her husband, he often found things to do with others on the weekends, leaving Caroline at home with their two young daughters. Caroline looked to friends and her children for the emotional connection she desired, given that she believed that her husband was not available or willing to meet her needs. Her actions, triggered by her negative thoughts, had caused great difficulty in the relationship. The resulting marital problems further reinforced the illusion Caroline had created that her husband was not committed to her.

Now that Caroline had insight into herself, she was able to be aware of and access the thoughts and beliefs that had been silently creating a life of perpetual suffering for her and those she loved. It was not until Caroline engaged in the simple practice of being with her thoughts that she became aware that she had not had actual choice in the past, and that these patterns had instead been running her life.

As a good friend of mine, who happened to also be a psychologist devoted to the betterment of others, once told me, "What I have come to realize after forty years of practice is that an awareness of a problem does not lead to the solution of that problem." Caroline was now aware of what was within her and how it was driving her. At this point, however, she still did not have access to new patterns and new ways of being and, therefore, was unable to choose anything outside of what she had already known.

Caroline then engaged in a program I designed where she developed the capacity to see what was operating even in the deepest levels of her mind, to sort through and identify those patterns that did not serve, and then to develop new thoughts, beliefs, and core concepts that align with what she wished to create. As a result of these new thought and belief patterns, Caroline now had access to new internal experiences. Through establishing these new internal patterns, Caroline acquired the ability to consciously choose a new way of existing within herself. This new way of existing then manifested a radically different life for Caroline. The practice that I gave Caroline, which allowed her to begin to change her life, was a basic, mindfulness meditation practice.

Although there are different types of meditation, the meditation that we will be practicing here is known as mindfulness meditation. Mindfulness meditation has been used extensively in scientific studies on meditation. The scientific support for mindfulness meditation's results is compelling. Practicing mindfulness trains the brain to achieve states of clarity, discipline, and mental focus. Being in such states facilitates awareness about the mind, creating opportunities for shifts and changes at a core level. Later in this book, we will provide techniques to get in touch with the emotions and shift out of reactive states by using this same type of meditation. However, disciplining the mind is the first step toward being able to develop a state of awareness that facilitates conscious choice as opposed to reaction based on our internal patterns. So this is where we start.

To begin mindfulness meditation, first find a quiet place. When meditating, always sit with the spine straight, either on the floor or in a chair, close the eyes, and breathe in and out through the nose. In this practice, your attention *is* on the breath. As you begin to breathe, focus on your *center*. Your center is located approximately two inches below the belly button and an inch back toward the spine. Gently inhale through the nose, drawing the breath into your lower abdomen while imagining a small golden sun in that space. Imagining a sun or a star in your center gives your mind something to focus on. Then just continue breathing *a circular breath*—breathing with as brief a pause at the top of the inhale or the bottom of the exhale as possible.

When you have a thought, acknowledge it: *That is my mind thinking a thought. The thought is not good or bad, positive or negative; it simply is an expression of energy created by my mind.* Then gently return your focus back to your center and your breath. Do not judge or become attached to what shows up in the mind; just be an observer of the mind's internal function. It is important to meditate for fifteen to twenty minutes a day. After you get proficient at this practice, you can then begin the process of *creating* your thoughts.

The goal of this meditation practice is to take the new awareness and tools developed there and apply them in your daily life. As Caroline did her practice over time, she was able to *show up* in her daily life with new thoughts, beliefs, and core patterns. Because she had awareness now of her own patterns and could stay present in the moment when these old patterns would surface, now she could shift and change out of them, choosing to create something different.

When thoughts would emerge based upon beliefs that her husband did not care for her and would one day abandon her, Caroline was able to redirect and focus her mind on the ways in which her husband was showing up for her and for their daughters. Caroline thought about the little things that her husband did in their everyday lives. She thought about how he picked their daughters up from after-school activities and fixed things around the house. She focused on how hard he tried at times to get her attention and to make her laugh. Each new thought pattern she was able to create opened new doors to other potential ways of thinking.

These new thought patterns began to support and build new belief structures for Caroline about her husband. *He doesn't care for me* and *he will leave me* were eventually replaced by beliefs that her husband *did* care for her and that he genuinely wanted to be with her. As her thought patterns and their supporting belief structures began to change, her relationship with her husband and their entire family dynamic shifted on all levels. The anger she had felt for her husband subsided and was replaced by genuine love and affection. Both Caroline and her husband had wished to provide a healthy and happy environment for their children but had been unable to do so. Now, their home was stable and warm, and their children thrived in their new-found environment.

Caroline, who had once been overly protective of her children, was now able to observe their independence with great pride. Instead of thinking that some catastrophic event would separate her from her beloved daughters, now she could stay present in the moment and fully enjoy whatever it was that they were experiencing. Instead of trying to restrain her daughters, she was able to enjoy their freedom. Thoughts such as *they are going to get hurt* were replaced by *look at them go*. For the first time, Caroline could vacation with her daughters and enjoy taking them boating, snorkeling, and parasailing without believing that the experience would end in disaster. Instead, she believed their adventures would create confidence in her daughters that would support the type of unburdened life that she wished her daughters to know and experience.

Caroline's professional career changed as well. Instead of obsessing about the risk inherent in her work and whether one day she would lose the money she made, she began to focus on the pleasure she took in supporting people and the contribution she believed that her work was making to the world. Instead of thinking that one day her financial world would crumble, she directed her thoughts to how people would be affected by what she was doing. When she began to focus her thoughts on the present and the work that she was doing in that moment, Caroline gained an increased proficiency at her job. As she ingrained positive thought patterns into her mind in connection with her work, she saw her practice becoming more and more successful. Her income increased, and her connection to her clients and those whom she worked with deepened substantially. Everything about Caroline's world had changed, and it now aligned with what she had wished to create all along.

The reason these practices were effective for Caroline was that she made a commitment to do them *consistently over a period of time.* When many people begin to meditate, they do it only for a short period of time or fail to implement the appropriate practices necessary to change the brain's neurology and establish a new way of being. The increasing body of science around meditation and its impact on the brain and neurology shows that a minimum of twenty minutes of daily practice over a period of even a few weeks is optimal for changing the habits and patterns that lie within.

When we make the commitment to master our minds, it is best to find a place where we can do our meditation practice daily. I tell my students that they need a place where there is as little distraction as possible. For example, you want a place where there is no television, no music, no children playing, and as little interruption as you can manage. Although we want a place that is as quiet and still as possible, we must work with what we have. If we live in a busy city, it is impossible to stop the traffic noise. If we live in an apartment building, there is nothing we can do about our disruptive neighbors. We do the best we can. With practice and in time, it will not matter what environment you do the work in. At the beginning, however, it is important to make the environment as supportive as possible for your daily practice.

Caroline admitted to me that when I originally gave her this task, the only place she could find that met my criteria was her closet. Although she lived in a large home, she quickly realized that almost the entire house was occupied with the frenetic energy of her husband and their two young children. The only place that was truly hers was her bedroom closet. As a result, she began to shut the door to her closet and meditate inside. Once she admitted to being what she called a "closet meditator," several of my other female clients admitted to doing the same thing. As funny as it may sound, this location worked well for them. I tell this story because *any space* will do as long it is a quiet space you use routinely where you won't be subject to interruption.

A primary reason to establish a consistent place to meditate daily is one that is grounded in neurology and the emerging body of science surrounding meditation. As we have been discussing, our brains learn through patterning. Therefore, when we establish a place we go to routinely to meditate, we begin to build a pattern in our brains. When we embark upon a meditative practice, we set out to construct new neuropathways in our brains that allow us to begin the process of mastering our minds. When we go to the same place over and over again to meditate, the brain recognizes that in this certain place we activate our new neuropathways for experiencing states beyond our known experiences.

During the last decade, science has taken an increasing interest in meditation. Because those who spend their lives in contemplative practices, such as monks and nuns, have reported experiencing states of deep peace, love, and joy through their practices, scientists wondered whether there was actually a physiological reason that meditators experienced these states of being that we would all like to achieve. If there was a neurological basis for these experiences, learning how to create these states would be of great service to our society.

With magnetic resonance imaging (MRI) or brain-scanning ability, medical professionals in the fields of neurology, neuropsychology, and neuroradiology began to study what meditation does to the structure and the function of the brain. These scientists compared the brains of meditators to the brains of those who do not meditate. As a result, we can now actually see inside the brains of meditators and view the impact meditation has on the brain. With what is called *functional* MRI or fMRI, these scientists can also watch how brains respond while a person is engaged in the process of meditating and document its results.

The National Institutes of Health, a medical research agency of the United States government, has now funded over 120 studies on meditation at many of the most prestigious universities and teaching hospitals, including Harvard, the University of Pennsylvania, Massachusetts General Hospital, UCLA, and MIT, to name a few. The body of science that has resulted from these studies uniformly supports meditation as a powerful tool for brain health and overall well-being on the mental, emotional, and physical levels. It is hard to think of another area of science where the outcomes of such a large and diverse number of studies have been so positive and compelling.

This body of scientific study proves that a small amount of daily meditation, in the range of fifteen to twenty minutes a day, actually alters the size of portions of the brain, the blood flow in the brain, and what parts of the brain are active in any given situation. In other words, there is now no doubt that meditation changes your brain and how it functions. There is also no doubt that these changes are for the better.

Daily meditation for a period of eight weeks has been shown to actually increase the physical size of the most evolved portion of our brains, the part that houses our capacity for love, compassion, and higher thoughts. This portion of the brain, known as the prefrontal cortex, also receives increased blood flow through routine meditation and begins to be more active in a wider range of circumstances. It is easy to imagine the impact that empowering the higher-functioning portions of our brains could have on our lives and on the world.

Among other things, what these studies show is that the brain, just like any muscle in the body, must be routinely exercised and trained if it is to achieve maximum function. Meditation is how we exercise our brain. In order to shift and change our minds, science has discovered that a daily meditation practice is critical. In this case, that exercise only takes a small time commitment of fifteen to twenty minutes every day.

Through a daily meditation practice, we learn to observe our minds and begin to break free. We become familiar with our thoughts and the beliefs underlying them as we spend time observing how our minds work. We also gain insight into what core concepts are operating deep within our unconscious minds. Over time, with routine practice, our ability to focus and direct our minds greatly increases. With this increased awareness and focus, our attachment to our conditioned mind begins to lessen, and therefore, so does the power of its patterns.

The untrained mind is a prison that entraps us within a maze of thoughts, beliefs, and concepts. As Gandhi said, "A man is but a product of his thoughts. What he thinks, he becomes." When we allow the mind to control us, it creates a mental prison that defines all aspects of our existence. The difficulty in breaking free from this mental prison is complicated by the mere fact that those enslaved do not even know they are trapped. So the irony is, if you are thinking that you are not entrapped by your mind, you most certainly are.

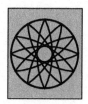

CHAPTER 4

The Dynamic Interaction between Mind and Emotion

Most people guard against going into the fire, and so end up in it.

—RUMI

Most of us are unaware of the dynamic and symbiotic connection between mind and emotion that makes our internal prison walls even more formidable. Often when people realize that their minds are negative and chaotic, they try using positive affirmations to *fix* their minds. In fact, it is in vogue today to give this prescription as a cure-all. The idea is that if one merely *thinks positively*, then the mind will shift and change to a positive state. However, changing the thoughts alone, without addressing their underlying belief structures and core concepts, is not effective. It is further doomed to fail because it overlooks the critical role that emotions play in concert with the mind. As a result, neither the mind nor the emotions are transformed.

Our emotions are the *energetic* foundation, supporting and fueling the direction our minds want to go. The emotions and the mind foster deep, interrelated connections. An emotional pattern triggers thoughts that are in alignment with that emotion. Those thoughts then fuel and sustain the emotion. The emotion then triggers more thoughts in alignment, and the emotion is bolstered again. Our thoughts and emotions literally feed off each other, revving each other up. Depending on the emotional pattern that is active, this relationship does not necessarily support our highest interests or overall well-being.

To further complicate the problem, many people are disconnected from their emotions and lack any awareness of how they actually feel. When we are not connected with how we feel, it is impossible to know how unseen emotions are driving our thoughts and our actions. Like the prison example from the previous chapter, any hidden pattern, be it mental or emotional, can imprison us. On the other hand, when the mind becomes well-trained and has the strength to influence the emotions, the mind has the potential to become the architect of our experience instead of the warden of our prison.

Having the ability to impact our emotional patterns is even more powerful and transformative than having the ability to redirect the mind. However, we cannot impact the emotions unless we have harnessed the mind first, because the trained mind is the tool we use to access and transform our emotions. Our tool for harnessing the power of the emotions begins with the mind because of the deep connection between the mind and the emotions. Therefore, it is critical that we develop a deep and accurate understanding of what emotions are and how they interact with the mind.

Like thought, every emotion is a vibration of energy. Each emotion exists along a spectrum of either divine love or fear. When we experience feelings aligning with fear, such as anger, hatred, jealousy, resentment, sadness, unworthiness, disgust, guilt, and shame, we set the emotional foundation to support and fuel thoughts of the same low vibration.

For example, the vibrational frequency of anger will create and fuel thoughts, beliefs, and concepts of a like nature, such as *I hate you; I don't want to see you again; you disrespected me;* and *you are wrong.* In turn, these thoughts will fuel and empower the vibration of anger, strengthening and reinforcing the pattern in our inner matrix. Each time we engage either the thought or the emotion, we are training the inner matrix to sustain, strengthen, and reinforce the pattern of anger inside us.

The same applies if we embody an emotion on the spectrum of divine love. When we experience feelings aligned with divine love, such as compassion, joy, serenity, peace, happiness, gratitude, forgiveness, tranquility, and passion, we set the emotional foundation to support and fuel thoughts of the same high vibration.

For example, the vibrational frequency of gratitude will create thoughts such as *I am so lucky; life is so wonderful; the universe is supporting my highest good;* and *it is a gift to be alive.* In turn, these thoughts will fuel and empower the vibration of gratitude, strengthening and reinforcing that pattern in our inner matrix. Each time we engage either the thought or the emotion, we are training the inner matrix to sustain, strengthen, and reinforce the pattern of gratitude inside us.

Emotions aligning with divine love cause our energy to expand, while emotions aligning with fear cause our energy to contract. Like the mind, in any given moment, our emotions are either operating and aligning with the aspect of divine love or fear, but never both. It is simply impossible for our emotions to be vibrating in a frequency of divine love and fear at the same time.

Until our mind is well-trained, emotions will trump our thoughts every single time. It is not even a fair fight. An example of this can be found by looking to the experience of one of my clients, Stacey. Stacey had experienced a history of betrayal in her life. When she was a young girl, she remembers her mother and father fighting because her father had been caught kissing another woman. What she later came to learn was that her father had an affair with this same woman.

Throughout Stacey's life, the men she had committed relationships with always ended up having affairs with other women. As a result, Stacey carried within her core emotional patterns of betrayal, insecurity, and jealousy. Stacey had a deep desire for a loving relationship with a significant other, but she had thoughts like M*en cannot be trusted, men can't control themselves, men are only interested in one thing, and men aren't capable of monogamy.* These thoughts were aligned with the vibrational frequency of Stacey's core emotional patterns of betrayal, insecurity, and jealousy. Because these thoughts and emotions are all aspects of fear, as Stacey engaged them over and over again, they had created a deep pattern of fear within Stacey's inner matrix. Ultimately fear permeated every aspect of Stacey's relationships and came to define her very existence.

Stacey eventually met a man, Blake, who was capable of a committed, monogamous relationship. This man cared deeply for Stacey. He respected her and thought the world of her. Unlike the other men she had been involved with, this man was not interested in pursuing other women and wanted only to be with her.

In the beginning of the relationship, everything was wonderful, but within a few short months, Stacey's internal patterns began to surface in response to coincidental events. Blake had become unable to call her as frequently as he would have liked due to an increase in his work schedule. He was also away more because his job was requiring him to travel to various cities. Each time Blake would leave town, upon his return, Stacey was certain that he had slept with another woman and would demand to know the details of the encounter. When Blake explained to Stacey that there was no other woman and that he was merely working, Stacey would become enraged, certain that he was lying to her about his trip.

In his apartment, Blake had several pictures of he and Stacey. It was not long before Stacey began asking Blake if he was taking the pictures of the two of them down and putting them back up only when Stacey visited his home. Stacey had noticed that from time to time, pictures of she and Blake seemed to have been moved a bit. Blake tried to explain that his cleaning woman probably moved the pictures when she dusted, but Stacey did not believe him. Instead, Stacey remained convinced that Blake was hiding the pictures of the two of them together in a drawer so that the other woman would not know of Stacey's relationship with Blake.

No matter how much Blake tried to reason with Stacey and reassure her that there was no other woman, Stacey would become more and more enraged, convinced Blake was lying. When Stacey's rage and insecurity would pass, she would come to realize that she had no proof that Blake had betrayed her or that Blake was interested in any other woman. Despite this fact, she would still not permit herself to trust him, because she believed it was only a matter of time until she did have the proof that there was another woman. Stacey simply could not allow the facts to interfere with her mental and emotional fantasy.

The other woman in Blake's life existed only in Stacey's fantasy but ended up destroying the relationship anyway. Stacey soon broke up with Blake, certain that he was having an affair. The reality of the situation was that Blake loved and respected Stacey and had been loyal to her throughout the time they were together. This is an example of how strong emotion can create our thoughts and beliefs, making pure fantasies a reality.

Emotion creates fantasies within our minds all the time. These fantasies are nothing more than the resurfacing of old mental and emotional patterns within the inner matrix. As we take action based on these fantasies, we take what is true only on the level of internal pattern and construct and manifest our external lives to mirror our internal patterns. This is how our inner world creates our outer reality.

If there is any question remaining as to whether our thoughts or emotions are more powerful, we need look no further than the advertising business to find an answer. Those who are in advertising know that emotion beats reason every single time. Every effective advertisement you can think of is selling an emotion as opposed to a product. Why is this the case? It is the power of emotion that determines and directs the actions we take—from the jobs we work, to the activities we engage in during our free time, to the people we choose to spend our time with, and even to the products we purchase.

A primary example is the old Coca Cola commercial where droves of people holding hands sang, "I'd like to teach the world to sing, in perfect harmony." Coca Cola was not selling a sugared soft drink in these commercials. Instead, they were selling world peace. Because we all desire to experience a peaceful state, despite the fact that we know sugary soft drinks are not healthy, we buy them anyway. Phillip Morris's Marlboro Man advertisements sold virility and masculinity. Although, lung cancer ultimately took the life of three of the Marlboro Man models, Marlboro cigarettes became the world's most highly sold tobacco brand of all time. Similarly, Nike's "Just Do It" campaign inspired people to purchase empowerment and confidence, not over-priced tennis shoes as it propelled Nike to the forefront of the athletic apparel market.

Pharmaceutical advertisements are certainly not selling intellectual reason. These advertisements show people who used to be depressed now experiencing love and acceptance while simultaneously listing all sorts of horrible things that can happen to those who use their products. If people were swayed by reason, these ads would not be effective, given the frequently gruesome side effects that are set forth in the ads. However, because emotion tops reason, these advertisements have cornered the airwaves and are among the most frequently shown on television today.

Another illustration of how a weak mind interacts with our emotions can be found in the earlier example of the New Year's resolution to get in shape. Despite our best initial intentions, we often find ourselves quitting our new workout regimen within a couple of months. As noted, the reason we quit is because we have a weak and undisciplined mind. However, it must be understood that the impulse to stop working out was not a thought that originated in the mind. It was an expanded feeling fathered in the emotional body and then *supported* by the mind. Whether we were aware of it or not, the emotional body engaged *first*.

Because working out doesn't feel particularly pleasurable after we have taken some time off, what happens is that the sensation of physical discomfort triggers the emotional body. We feel pain. Our muscles ache. We begin to have a negative emotional response to what we intellectually know is serving us. We may feel frustrated that we have to spend time at the gym when we would rather be home with a lover, spouse, friends, or children. Sometimes we start to feel sorry for ourselves. Perhaps we feel shame that we haven't been to the gym in a long time and that we look so out of shape. One way or another, the impulse to stop working out is an emotional reaction. Our mind gets involved by justifying and supporting the emotion to take action that otherwise does not make sense, given that routine exercise is important to our health.

Because the emotions drive the mind, if we do not shift the emotional vibration supporting our thoughts, beliefs, and concepts, even if we think positive and affirmative thoughts, the emotions will dominate those thoughts. Our minds are not capable of holding ground in a state of rational thought when faced with an emotional onslaught.

If we have awareness that counterproductive emotional activity is undermining our vision, we can direct our mind to thoughts like, *This may hurt now, but soon I will see the benefits of going to the gym,* or *even If it is not pleasurable, working out now is critical so I won't become sick later.* However, if we have not developed emotional awareness, our emotions will override our minds and continue to dictate our actions.

For example, if we feel overwhelmed, stressed, fatigued, bored, or insecure, and we are unaware of the existence of these emotional patterns and how to shift them, these emotions will covertly undermine and sabotage the mind. Because the emotions direct the mind, the mind will find a way to justify why it was appropriate for our destructive actions to align with our emotions. Despite our best efforts, we will find ourselves once again stopping our exercise routine. In order to shift our emotions, we must first understand what they are and how they operate.

Emotions, like everything else in this human experience, are just energy. The emotional patterns we experience throughout our lives are learned energetic imprints most of which were developed even before we could speak. Because we cannot identify emotion without thought, we cannot think without language, and we require language to define our feelings, our core emotional patterns go unidentified, hidden deep within the recesses of our unconscious self.

If our mothers were happy, the vibration of happiness was imprinted within our emotional bodies. When we were born, we began to absorb the emotional patterns of those caring for us as well. As a result, if our fathers or those around us were angry, the vibration of anger was imprinted within our emotional bodies. We then replay these emotional patterns over and over throughout our lives. However, we often lack any conscious awareness of why we feel what we feel.

The reason we lack emotional awareness can be found in understanding how our brains develop. From the time of conception until typically around the age of two, our minds cannot think, because thinking is a process that requires language, and language is not a skill we possess at this developmental phase. As a result, we experience the world through the undefined energetic vibration otherwise known as emotion. These emotional patterns are undefined because we do not have language to identify them. At this point in our development, these undefined emotional vibrations are the only way we have to relate to the world around us and our only means of self-expression. Although an infant cannot talk, as we all know, an infant can certainly experience and express emotion.

These experiences of the world by way of emotional patterns are our first experiences of life, and as a result, they become imprinted deep within our developing unconscious self. The reason these early energetic emotional experiences are imprinted in our unconscious is because our developing brain only has the unconscious mind to imprint upon. At this point, we are not *conscious*. An infant lacks the brain waves necessary to create a subconscious or a conscious mind. Therefore, the unconscious is the only place these emotional experiences can be stored.

From birth to two years, at the time when typically there is no language, the human brain predominantly operates at the lowest EEG frequency, known as *delta waves*. As Taylor and Rutter note in *Child and Adolescent Psychology*, studies have shown that delta waves still appear during waking times of even five-year-olds. Delta waves are the waves produced by the unconscious brain. As a result, the early emotional energetic experiences we encounter are laid down through delta waves in our unconscious minds, where we lack access to them.

A University of Oregon study examined the impact of an infant's environment on the developing brain and its emotional patterning. The purpose of the study was to determine how and when a stressful experience leaves its mark on a developing brain. Researchers surveyed parents of six to twelve month old infants to determine the level of anger in their environment. The parents put the infants to sleep. The researchers put headphones on them and placed them into an fMRI machines. The headphones delivered recordings of nonsense phrases read in both neutral and angry voices. The researchers charted the response of the sleeping infants' brains to the gibberish being played through the headphones. The results showed that babies whose parents fought frequently in the home had a stronger neurological response to the angry sounding noises as compared to infants from homes with less conflict. The study also showed an impact in brain regions involved in processing stress, leading researchers to conclude that such exposure to anger could lead to problems later in life with handling frustration. As noted in a Smithsonian, October 2013 article discussing the study "the new research underscores the view that little brains are incredibly impressionable."

By the age of twelve, our brain predominantly enters the state of *beta waves,* which are associated with normal waking consciousness. Beta waves are the hallmark of the average, adult brain function as we go through our everyday lives. When we are in a beta state, we have little or no access to the delta waves that formed our unconscious mind and that house our core emotional patterns. After we pass into our teenage years, we can only access delta states during our deepest levels of sleep. Because this inaccessible delta state is where our core emotional patterning is stored, we lack an awareness of what emotions lie *deep* within. Because our unconscious mind stores our earliest emotional patterns, these patterns are the most powerful. As we create our life's experiences from our core emotional patterns, we are not consciously aware that we either carry these patterns or that they in fact create our experience.

Therefore, our earliest emotional imprints act like ghosts within us, silently influencing all aspects of our lives. We are unaware of their presence as they haunt our inner matrix and silently direct our thoughts and actions. Although we are often aware of some of our emotional patterns, those that are most powerful and assert the greatest influence over our lives are buried deep within our unconscious, hidden from our awareness.

Because emotions are primarily learned patterns and no two people have the exact same life experiences, everyone has a different emotional range due to their individualized imprinted patterns. This is why no two people will necessarily have the same emotional reaction to a given situation.

For example, many people have a very strong reaction about getting up and speaking in front of an audience. In fact, polls routinely show that fear of speaking in public ranks higher than fear of flying, illness, or terrorism. In some polls, the fear of speaking in public ranks even higher than the fear of death. Comedian Jerry Seinfeld's famous joke was that "at a funeral, the average person would rather be in the casket than giving the eulogy." Clearly this is not a rational response, but instead a powerful emotional reaction.

Even though most of us do not know anyone who has been either seriously injured or died as a result of a speaking engagement, if we had shy parents and did not receive certain emotional imprints as a child, speaking in front of a group would be terrifying. For those of us who encountered situations where we were humiliated or embarrassed in front of a group of people, we will most likely have strong emotional reactions against public speaking. If we were shamed when we spoke up by being told that children were to be seen and not heard, we may also have a negative emotional reaction to expressing our opinions publicly.

If, on the other hand, we had very outgoing parents and were placed in situations as children where we had to exercise certain emotional skills, then we might feel comfortable speaking in front of a group. If we received positive emotional feedback when we found ourselves at the center of attention, we might love to stand in front of an audience. Instead of being terrified, we might be exhilarated by the experience. Unlike our counterparts, we have a constructive emotional pattern tied to public expression.

Contrary to popular thought, there is no right or wrong emotional reaction to any given experience in our lives. As this example shows, emotion is not an objective system that is uniform from one person to the next. Two people can have completely divergent experiences of the same factual situation. How we react to the external circumstances of our lives depends on the emotional imprints contained within our inner matrix.

As human beings, we are capable of experiencing a wide range of emotions, but most of us experience a limited range. Take a moment and see how many emotions you can quickly identify as having experienced today. Most people are surprised by the limited number of emotions that spring to their minds. The reason we cannot quickly identify a large range of emotional experiences is that we replay the same set of imprinted emotional patterns over and over again. Most people are unable to experience a wide range of emotions until they have engaged practices to evolve their emotional capacity.

When we experience the same emotions over and over again, these patterns become stronger and stronger over time, making them very powerful. Every time we trigger a familiar emotional pattern, it becomes more and more entrenched in us just like the rut in the snow that we previously discussed. It is important to understand that an emotion is like a living being that demands to be fed in order to sustain itself and grow. What an emotion feeds on is more of that same emotional energy. For example, if we routinely feel anger, the pattern of anger requires more and more anger to feed and sustain our growing emotional pattern. The more we feed the anger, the stronger it becomes, and the more it demands to be fed. As a result, anger will escalate in our lives, we will feel anger more frequently, and its intensity will increase.

Because the energy of anger needs to be fed to stay active within us, we will unconsciously create situations in our lives that will trigger the pattern of anger inside of us. When we carry the pattern of anger, our mind creates thoughts, beliefs, and concepts to rationalize being angry. So when we look at our spouse, children, jobs, and friends through this mental lens driven by the emotion of anger, it provides us with justification for being angry. This emotional food, so to speak, may look like a husband yelling at his wife over mundane issues. It can also appear as becoming irritated or even enraged when someone cuts us off in traffic. When something doesn't go well at work, we become angry at those we believe to be responsible for the situation. These examples are fairly easy to recognize as fodder for anger.

If anger is driving our minds to create thoughts, beliefs, and concepts that validate our anger, then we will experience anger over and over again. Therefore, it is reasonable that the energy of anger will attract people into our lives who also carry the energy of anger. Those who share our emotional energetic patterns will be attracted to and resonate with us, while those who do not carry our emotional energetic patterns will not. A person who carries the energy of joy will not want to spend time in our space.

On the other hand, when we are with people who carry the energy of anger, we support each other's inner emotional patterns. We get angry at each other. We complain about the world. We lament about how we are angry because of what other individuals have done to us. Through this interaction, our emotional patterns of anger are fed and reinforced.

This phenomenon has actually been measured on a physiological level by modern neurology. In the 1990s, neuroscientists discovered what are now known as *mirror neurons.* The discovery happened by accident in a lab in Parma, Italy. In the lab, monkeys were implanted with electrodes to monitor brain activity. A neurologist was watching how a monkey's brain fired when the monkey would pick up a nut, crack it open, and eat it.

While the monkey's brain was being monitored, a lab technician walked into the lab and picked up one of the nuts, cracked it open, and ate it. As the monkey merely watched this lab technician, the pattern in the monkey's brain that controlled picking up a nut, cracking it open, and eating it functioned as though the monkey was engaging in the action himself. The monkey had not moved. He had not done a thing. Instead, all that happened was that the monkey watched the lab technician. By watching the actions occur, the monkey experienced the same brain activity as if the monkey had been the one acting. This is the phenomenon of mirror neurons.

As a result of our mirror neurons, as far as our brains are concerned, watching someone doing something is the same as doing it ourselves. Our mirror neurons cannot tell the difference. They fire as though we are doing the activity that we are only seeing. Neuroscientists now believe that mirror neurons are a critical tool in learning. They are the scientific explanation for the old saying about small children, "Monkey see, monkey do." Mirror neurons are why and how children learn through imitation.

However, it is important to note that mirror neurons remain active throughout our adult life.

Mirror neurons also are what provide us with the capacity for empathy. Because our brains have the ability to mirror the experiences of those around us, we are able to feel empathy for others. In an empathetic state, we experience the emotions of others as though they were our own—*and in that experience, they become our own.*

Therefore, when we watch someone experience an emotion, we experience it as well. Scientists have conducted studies where they put study participants into an fMRI brain-scanning machine and showed them pictures of other people's faces. In the pictures, the people were experiencing various emotions and making the facial expressions consistent with those emotions. When the study participants looked at the pictures, their brains showed activity in the areas corresponding to the emotions displayed in the pictures. For example, if the person in the picture looked angry, then the study participant's brain showed activity in the region controlling anger. The participants also reported feeling the same emotion as was shown in the picture.

Through mirror neurons, we connect and reinforce emotional patterns within each other. So if the emotional patterns that have been conditioned in our brains resonate most strongly with anger, we will most easily connect with other people in a place of anger. When the other person we are connecting with gets angry, then we have the experience of anger through our mirror neurons, and our own pattern of anger is fed. If an emotional pattern of joy within our brain has been reinforced, then we will connect most easily with others who are joyful. When the person we are connecting with becomes joyful, then we have the experience of joy through our mirror neurons, and our own pattern of joy is fed.

Knowing how our emotional patterns came to exist within us, the role emotions play in creating the experience of our day-to-day lives, and the fact that emotions, like thoughts, are just energy, we begin to form a foundation for building a healthy relationship with our emotions. Once we have this understanding, we can learn how to utilize emotion as a tool to create more dynamic and joy-filled lives.

As we take steps toward building a relationship with our emotions, we must first understand clearly the role healthy emotion is to play in our lives. Emotion is often mistaken as being intuition. When we experience an emotion, we must realize that this is not some divine or higher communication. In our society, emotion is frequently seen as an internal guidepost that will lead us in the right direction when we don't know which way to turn. Think about how many times someone has asked you "But how do you *feel* about it?" when you were trying to make an important life-changing decision such as getting married, selecting the college you would attend, or deciding what career to pursue. Most of us have even asked others this same question when they were pondering a difficult decision. We've been told or educated to *trust our gut*.

The premise behind the question "how do you feel about it?" is that we should follow our feelings. This strategy is an uneducated recipe for disaster in all aspects of our lives and, particularly, in our relationships. We are not our emotions. Emotion simply is not an objective or trustworthy navigational system. One thing we must know for certain is that using emotion as a personal GPS will get us stranded in a bad neighborhood instead of leading us home.

Because emotion is primarily learned behavior, we cannot think of our emotions as pointing which way to turn in the present moment. Instead, we must see our emotions as maps of where we have been in the past. If we pay attention, we can see that our emotions are responsible for bringing us to where we are in this current moment. Therefore, if we wish to make changes in our lives, we must gain access to different emotional patterns so that these new patterns bring us to a different place and experience in the future. Emotions are the programs we used to create our past experiences. Like Stacey, if we continue to rely on these same emotional patterns, they will create the same experience in our present, which guarantees that our future life experiences will be identical to our past.

When we engage the same emotional patterns over and over again, our world looks the same, day after day. The people in our world may change. We may not live in the same houses, drive the same cars, or have the same partners, but our experience of the world is very much the same, because emotionally we are stagnant. We may wish to experience relationships and careers that are more fulfilling, but no matter what we change on the outside, on the inside, our experience will be the same if we do not shift and change our emotional patterns.

If our lives are not perfect and we wish to create something new, different, and magnificent, we do not *follow* our emotions. Instead, we learn how to harness them. When we acquire this skill, we direct emotion as a tool to fuel and create our visions instead of allowing emotion to covertly direct our lives according to old, conditioned patterns.

Even if we are happy and content in our lives, this does not mean that we do not wish to create new and different experiences. The question is whether we want our tomorrows to look like our yesterdays. We may feel perfectly fulfilled. Our lives may be quite happy. We may enjoy good relationships with our spouses, coworkers, children, and friends. At the same time, we may wish to grow and deepen our emotional range so that we can have expanded experiences in this life. We may have a desire to realize our unmanifested potentials, knowing that we are capable of more. We may just be curious about other ways of being and what is possible for us to create in this life. Evolving our emotional intelligence will enhance the current experience of our lives, either making the bad good or the good better.

An example of being driven by emotion that many people can relate to can be found where a couple breaks up only to get back together again. Often, when couples separate, they are experiencing emotions of deep anger and hurt and choose to separate as a result of that pain. As time passes, the emotional intensity temporarily lessens or dissolves and the couple begins to question whether they made a mistake by leaving the relationship.

The emotion of loneliness surfaces, causing them to think of the "good times" they had and to consider salvaging the relationship. The two believe they made a mistake by separating. Since anger is not currently present, they both believe they have changed. They are not aware that their emotional patterns are still driving their actions. They believe "it will be different this time," although neither one has done the deep work necessary to shift the emotional patterns that got them into trouble in the first place.

The old relationship feels comfortable because the destructive emotional patterns that played out in the relationship were the same patterns that had continually replayed throughout their lives. As a result, these emotional patterns are familiar, and what is familiar feels comfortable. These patterns are all that the couple has ever known and all that they are capable of accessing. Believing that things will be different this time, the couple decides to give it a go again. Of course, after a while, their old patterns rear their ugly heads. Because the imprinted emotional patterns are the same, so is the experience of the relationship.

If the couple doesn't get back together and, instead, one of the partners engages in a new relationship, the experience of this new relationship, with a different person, will actually be the same as with the original partner. Our experience is simply not tied to the person whom we broke up with. Instead, it is generated by the emotional patterns buried deep within us. As a result, the new relationship serves as a vehicle to trigger our internal emotional patterns, and since the same emotional patterns inside us are being fed, our experience of the new relationship becomes like our experience of the old one. We can run from relationships, but we cannot hide from ourselves. Because we take ourselves wherever we go, if we wish to transform our lives, we must transform the inner matrix.

In order to move out of destructive emotional patterns that are creating pain and suffering in our lives, we must become aware that the patterns exist and know when they are influencing our lives. To get in touch with our emotions, an important first step is to begin checking in with your emotions several times a day. Set an alarm on your phone or watch to remind yourself to check in with your emotions. When your alarm goes off, take a moment, tune into how you are feeling, and acknowledge what is present within your emotional body. Then give yourself ninety seconds to simply *be with* whatever emotion is present, experiencing it fully.

As you become aware of the emotion present for you in the moment, do not judge the feeling. Just be with the emotion. Accept the emotion and give the emotion permission to express fully within you. Remember, no matter what emotional experience comes up, it is okay to feel the emotion. It is okay to be angry, sad, and lonely, just as it is okay to be joyful, happy, and peaceful. No emotion is good or bad. It is healthy and normal to feel emotion. Emotions are normal human expressions.

If you can't find or identify what you are feeling, do not judge that experience either. Just keep doing the practice, and in time, the emotions will reveal themselves to you. Just like our thoughts, our emotions do not always want to be seen, and sometimes, they hide from us when we focus on them. The good news is, if you embark upon this daily practice, your emotions cannot hide forever.

In our quest not to judge the emotions that we are experiencing in any given moment, it helps to remember that emotions are just energy and that we are now developing the tools to address them. There is nothing to be afraid of where our emotions are concerned. *We are not our emotions.* Repeat: we are not our emotions, and therefore, we are neither more nor less as a result of the emotional experiences we are having in any given moment. We can look our emotions in the face and allow them to fully express inside of us without judgment. If we merely allow emotions to flow through us without resistance, they will quickly pass.

In fact, emotions will *always* pass if they are allowed to. A Harvard neuroanatomist by the name of Jill Bolte Taylor has written a fascinating story about her experience of having a massive stroke and her subsequent eight-year recovery process. She cites that scientific research has shown that the neurological life of an emotion is ninety seconds if we do not fuel it with thoughts, beliefs, and concepts that feed it. It appears that our mothers' advice to breathe and count to ten before acting was actually grounded in an intuitive understanding of what science has now proven.

Each time you experience an emotion, the brain produces and releases a cocktail of neurochemicals associated with that emotion. These neurochemicals are called neurohormones and neuropeptides. For example, when you are angry, the brain produces the combination of neurohormones and neuropeptides associated with anger. These neurochemicals rush into the brain and then race out into the rest of the body.

The good news is that left on their own, these neurochemicals have short life spans. The bad news is that our reasoning is momentarily clouded because our brain is swimming in a flood of these powerful chemicals. The experience is akin to being momentarily under the influence of a drug like cocaine. With an understanding of brain chemistry, it's easy to see why we get into trouble when we follow our emotions and why we actually get addicted to our emotional patterns.

It is important to note that it is not just the emotions we might classify as negative—such as anger, grief, depression, and shame—that have the power to overwhelm us. Emotions that we think of as positive can also overwhelm our brain. Science has now shown that there is a reason that we often identify those early stages of romantic love as being "madly in love." Infatuation has the power to make us crazy through the same process that anger does.

Dr. Helen Fisher, an anthropology professor at Rutgers University, has researched the chemicals that flood our brains when we experience initial romantic infatuation. Dr. Fisher used brain-imaging equipment to see what happened in the brains of volunteers who looked at pictures of those with whom they were infatuated. What she discovered was that the areas of the brain that lit up were the same ones as those corresponding to drug addiction.

In particular, the brain experienced the same neurological response to infatuation that it did to taking cocaine. Those participants who were experiencing infatuation experienced sleeplessness and a loss of a sense of time. They also experienced an almost obsessive-compulsive focus on the one they loved, even to their own detriment. Dr. Fisher concluded that the chemicals produced when we are in a state of infatuation simply overwhelm the rational thinking process with the same force and through the same mechanism as cocaine and other dangerously powerful drugs.

The neurohormones and neuropeptides that seize control of our brain, whether they are associated with anger, love, or any other emotion, then rush into our system and exert a powerful force on our physical bodies as well. These chemicals, once released into the body, actually lock into receptor sites on our cells. As a result, our emotions get physically trapped in our bodies' nervous systems. Therefore, even after the initial rush is gone, what was created as a result of that emotional experience remains in our physical bodies. This science explains why there is a very strong connection between our minds, our emotions, and our physical health.

The connection is not directly between the mind and the body. The direct connection is between the emotions and the body. The emotions trigger the chemical response that gets locked into the cells. Our thoughts may fuel the emotions and cause them to have significantly longer staying power than their natural life of ninety seconds, but the thoughts are not the root of the problem or pattern. The thoughts are only the symptom of the underlying emotion.

By stopping and taking ninety seconds to acknowledge our emotions and allow them to freely express, we develop a greater awareness and sensitivity about how we are feeling moment-to-moment. As a result, the grip our emotions hold on us is lessened. Like the mind where the thoughts are no longer thinking us, we begin to create a space where the emotions are no longer driving us. Instead, we begin to direct the emotions. Because of the power of our emotions, this easy practice provides us with a powerful tool to begin to transform our lives.

* * *

Bill is an executive in a high-powered corporation. Bill and his wife, Barbara, had been married for almost twenty years but found their way to me because their relationship was coming to an end. When they first came to one of my weekend programs, Bill said that he didn't mean to put any pressure on me, but that they were filing for divorce by the end of the weekend if I couldn't help their relationship.

Bill and Barbara were extremely angry individuals who had been unknowingly feeding the anger in each other for years. Bill's constant state of frustration and anger made it impossible for him to see how to solve the issues coming up in his relationship with his wife. Bill and Barbara's attempts to discuss their marital difficulties either ended in yelling and screaming matches or with Bill withdrawing to his garage to work on his cars and contemplate how the entire situation was Barbara's fault.

Bill also brought his frustration and anger to the workplace and the many teams of employees he supervised. When these teams failed to perform as Bill anticipated, Bill's pattern of anger was triggered. Bill would become defensive, blaming his employees for the shortcomings, threatening to fire them, writing them up, and even yelling and screaming at them.

As a result of the anger that permeated his life, Bill found himself constantly tired and stressed. Bill began to suffer from high blood pressure. He had difficulty sleeping at night because his mind obsessed about how he could solve the multitude of issues in both his professional and personal lives and who was to blame. Although Bill could not see it, his problems were not his wife, his team, or the multitude of other situations he encountered that made him angry. Bill was unaware that anger had seized him, becoming his inner tyrant and controlling his every thought, emotion, and action. Bill believed that his situation was unique, based upon what had shown up in his external world. In reality, Bill was merely taking predictable action based on the *intelligence of anger.*

Every emotion has a level of intelligence and a predictable way in which it functions within us. For example, when the pattern of anger is triggered, as much as we would like to think otherwise, we become very predictable. Think of the last time you became angry. What were the symptoms physically, mentally, and emotionally that showed up? Think about the last time that your spouse, business associate, or friend became angry. What showed up for them? Because of the mirror neurons and neurochemicals we discussed before, how anger presents itself and drives one person is the same as it is for another. No matter who is feeling anger, the feeling, the symptoms, and the actions we take are the same.

One reason some of us like to feel angry is that it feels powerful. Although anger is truly not a powerful state, as the adrenaline produced by anger courses through our bodies, we feel very powerful in that moment. Our heart races, our blood pressure rises, our body tenses, and our temperature rises. These are all symptoms of anger's intelligence. When anger is present, we also become very defensive, and we move into a place where we blame others. Regardless of the situation and the happenings around us, we are always correct: "I am right and you are most definitely wrong." When we are angry, we step into a state of righteousness.

When we become angry, we also either become loud—yelling and screaming as a way of attacking those around us—or we shut down, storming out of the room or withdrawing as a way of fleeing. When anger is present, we enter a state of *fight or flight*, aligning ourselves with fear. When we are in such a state of fear, we are no longer in control of our actions. Anger is the driving force instead. Our primal survival instinct takes over, and we are no longer capable of taking rational action. Clearly, this is not a state of self-empowerment.

When we think back to times when we have been angry, sending out caustic emails or saying unkind things to those we love, we become aware of anger's destructive impact. Almost always, after the initial surge of anger dies down and we have time to reflect on the actions we have taken, we have a sense of regret, embarrassment, and shame about what we did or said while we were angry. Just like we do "stupid" things when our brains are under the influence of alcohol, we also do "stupid" things when we are under the influence of anger. The same basic neurological process is active in creating both experiences.

Although most of us wish to choose a conscious and thoughtful response in the face of intense emotion, we simply do not know how to do so. None of us wish to act in an unintelligent and irrational manner, but that is the intelligence of anger at work. In laymen's terms, when we are angry, we are *stupid*.

I frequently provide a mantra to begin to reverse the potentially destructive tide of our emotional reactions to anger. I tell my students that when we feel angry, we need to stop, breathe, and say over and over, "I am angry. Therefore, in this moment, I am stupid. I will take no action." Although it sounds a little harsh, it takes such a harsh message to get through the haze of emotional drugs clouding our brains.

This practice is effective because it is grounded in what neuroscience has discovered about how we operate. Just breathing and doing nothing until the flood of neurochemicals has passed will allow us to regain a sense of clarity before we think, speak, or take action. Remember, all we need is ninety seconds. When our minds are clear, and we step out of the destructive emotional pattern, our intelligence significantly increases, allowing us to once again make a clear and rational decision about what conscious action to take. In this way, we begin to make choices that serve us instead of engaging a destructive emotional reaction.

When we take a moment to breathe, we are also interrupt our ingrained neurological patterns and actually begin to create new patterns in our brains. As we discussed previously, in order to survive, emotions need to be fed. Therefore, in order to establish a new emotional pattern that can trump the old one, we need to starve the old pattern and engage the new.

Through his work with these principles, Bill began to see that both his professional and marital issues were rooted in the fact that he had no access to or ways to navigate his emotions. As a result, Bill had no idea what was driving his actions. Bill had a childhood resembling what many young boys experience. When Bill would fall down and skin his knee, he was told not to cry. Bill was taught that it was not masculine for men to express their emotions. In fact, no one in Bill's family talked of their emotions.

Bill grew up believing that it was normal not to express emotion, and over time, he cut himself off from his emotions. As a result, Bill moved into his mind. In many ways, living in his mind served Bill while he was in school. Developing his intellectual abilities served him in his professional life as well. However, his inability to experience his emotions was a disaster for his personal life and ultimately weakened his professional acumen as well.

I gave Bill the practice of checking in with his emotions several times a day. Bill was certain that he was fine and that this practice held nothing for him. However, in a matter of a few short weeks, Bill came to realize that he was angry and had no control over his anger. The fact was, Bill's pattern of anger was controlling him and defining all aspects of his life.

Prior to doing the practice, Bill had absolutely no awareness of how the pattern of anger was driving him and the impact it was having on his life. As we have said, it is very difficult for us to see ourselves, and Bill was no exception to this rule. Once Bill could see the impact and intelligence of anger, Bill could recognize that anger was not supporting him to create a loving relationship with his wife or a high-functioning workplace. Bill began to see that anger disconnected him from accessing his very high level of intelligence.

By simply engaging the process of checking in with his emotions and being with them, Bill began to develop conscious choice instead of the illusion of choice. Before this practice, Bill had no ability to choose his actions, even though taking action from that place of anger was hurting those he loved and those he worked with. This simple practice gave him the ability in the moment to acknowledge that he was angry, step out of the anger, and choose a new place from which to take action.

Another aspect of anger that Bill came to recognize was how anger drove his mind to create fantasies and stories about reality that simply did not exist. When anger was present for Bill, which was quite frequently, his mind created stories that justified his angry state and allowed the anger to persist well beyond its otherwise limited lifespan of ninety seconds. Bill's mind told him that his employees were incompetent and lazy, incapable of performing to the level he desired. Bill's mind told him that his wife was ungrateful and that she was incapable of truly caring for him and his needs. Secretly, Bill feared that he was not able to hold his marriage together or perform at work, and as a result, there must be something fundamentally wrong with him.

All of these stories were generated by Bill's mind to justify, support, and further fuel his pattern of anger. None of these stories had much of a basis in reality. The truth was that Bill was a highly successful executive surrounded by teams of competent workers who almost always hit their marks. Bill's wife genuinely loved and respected him and was committed to making their relationship work. Bill could not see these realities because he was looking through the lens of anger, blinded by the stories his mind had created, trapping him in a life of needless suffering.

As Bill continued the practice of checking in with his emotions and implementing the ninety-second rule, Bill began to step out of the pattern of anger. As a result, he became aware of and in touch with other emotional patterns previously inaccessible to him. Bill began to see the emotional ghosts within his inner matrix and how they had been influencing and defining every aspect of his life. Bill discovered that underneath his anger were the ghosts of betrayal, insecurity, sadness, unworthiness, shame, and guilt that had all aligned him with fear. When he could see these once-invisible patterns, Bill began to make new choices in his daily life. Bill chose to create new emotional patterns within his inner matrix that aligned him with aspects of love instead of fear.

As Bill began to construct new emotional patterns of love, joy, peace, and compassion, he began to consciously transform his inner matrix and to create a substantially better life for himself and those around him. Bill's relationship with his wife dramatically improved. Bill is now capable of showing up for his wife with love and compassion, which were states not previously available to him. Bill no longer feels defensive or the need to either yell at or withdraw from his wife. As a result, Bill and his wife are able to communicate. This increased level of communication has forged a deep connection between them.

Bill's relationships at work have improved as well, which has fostered a new level of productivity and teamwork in his professional environment. Because Bill is no longer in a place of blame, Bill has been able to establish a sense of teamwork and camaraderie with his employees.

Bill is no longer obsessive about the issues in his life. As a result, his mind is able to be in a place of increased stillness. He is finally able to get a good night's sleep. Bill's overall state of health has improved, and he finds himself in a state of renewed vitality.

When we wish to step into a new way of being and dramatically change our lives, as Bill did, we must remember that the most important thing is to practice a new way of feeling and taking action in our lives until it becomes our default. We should not be too hard on ourselves when, in the beginning, we regress back to old emotional patterns. These old emotional patterns were fed and nourished over a long time and therefore, it takes them a while to dissolve. However, as we feed and nourish new emotional patterns, these grow in strength and soon become our new defaults.

If we sit with an emotion for more than ninety seconds and the emotion either does not dissolve or becomes stronger, then the mind is fueling the emotion through story. The emotion drives the mind to take simple facts that have shown up in the world and build a fantasy to justify and support the emotion that we are experiencing. The mind's storytelling provides the emotion with the ability to *stick* and stay in the present moment.

We can think of *story* as a type of neurological adhesive. If we tell ourselves a story, then our emotions have staying power for more than ninety seconds. Now our brain has given our emotions permission to fuel an emotional experience that otherwise might have passed. Now we are trapped in a pattern. When we repeat these stories over and over to ourselves, we begin to form physical, neurological pathways in the brain connected to these stories. When the pathway is triggered, the emotion will reemerge, getting stronger each time we fall back into this neurological rut.

As Bill engaged the practice of emotional transformation, he began to see the role of story in his life. One day as Bill was walking through the plant, he noticed an employee standing by himself staring into space. In this moment, Bill regressed back to his old pattern of anger. His mind began to create a story, fueled by anger, about this employee. He immediately began to criticize the employee in his head, thinking the employee was lazy and wasting time when there was a critical deadline to meet. Bill was convinced that the employee was purposefully trying to sabotage Bill, given that Bill and not the employees were penalized when deadlines were not met. Bill began to walk toward the employee to yell at him for being lazy and to tell him to get back to work.

Suddenly, Bill remembered to take a moment, tune in to how he was feeling, and do his ninety-second practice. Upon tuning in, Bill realized that he was angry and frustrated. He realized that his old pattern of anger was driving his mind to create the story about a lazy employee. As a result, Bill shifted his emotional state to his new pattern of peace.

Once he was in this new state, Bill walked toward the employee. As Bill approached the employee, the employee was excited to share his news with Bill that he had just completed a major project and had finished well ahead of his deadline. The employee was merely taking a break to clear his head. Bill congratulated the employee on a job well done.

In that moment, Bill realized that before he began doing his emotional work, employees had scurried away from him when they had seen him coming. No one had felt safe to confide in Bill because of his anger. Now, Bill had a connection with those he worked with. Bill realized the damage that his anger could have had on this employee and their relationship had he accused him of being lazy when, in actuality, he had performed with excellence. Bill expressed to me how grateful he was that he was able to control his anger and bring his new state of peace to the workplace.

We all unknowingly create stories as a result of emotional ghosts driving our minds. For example, many of us have had someone we love fail to acknowledge an important day, such as our birthday or anniversary, in the manner we expected. When we realize the day has come and gone and that our loved one did not meet our expectations, we may initially feel hurt and angry.

If we sit with that emotion and the facts as they have actually shown up, the experience will quickly pass. Once we have given the intense emotion permission to express itself fully without resistance and the emotion has then dissipated, we can address the issue with our loved one and discuss the facts. However, if we allow our mind to create a story around the event, our ability to deal with the factual situation goes right out the window. Now we are lost in a realm where our emotional pattern fuels the mind and the mind in return feeds the emotional pattern by creating fantasy.

One fantasy that the mind might create when fueled with the emotional patterns of sadness, rejection, and unworthiness is that our loved one just doesn't appreciate us. In fact, this oversight becomes *prima facie* evidence that the person does not truly love us. If that person appreciated us and loved us, he or she would have shown up differently. He or she would know that this was an important day and would have acted accordingly. How can we continue to be with someone who so obviously does not care about our feelings? The only conclusion that we can draw is that our loved one is certainly a callous person to have hurt us in this way.

It is clear that if your mind is allowed to create such a story, the experience will not be gone in under two minutes. Instead, the mind will play the story over and over again, feeding the emotional patterns of unworthiness, rejection, and sadness, while strengthening them in the process. This issue will grow and expand, taking on a life of its own in the relationship and creating havoc and suffering for yourself and someone you love. It is important when looking at this example to see clearly how little of the story is actually factual. Please understand that this is how story operates, allowing the mind to fuel the emotions.

Most of the stories our minds create are mere fairy tales. Very little, if any, of the stories about ourselves, others, and our lives are actually based on fact. Unfortunately, we adopt our stories as truth, and the stories become our reality. Our emotional patterns direct the mind to write the stories that become our lives.

There is no way to create and manifest the lives we desire by attempting to navigate the fictitious stories that our minds created from emotional patterning. Our society teaches that if we change the story and external circumstances of our lives, we will alleviate our discomfort. This is pure fiction.

Because the story is operating at the level of the conscious mind as a mere symptom of our underlying emotional pattern, working to change the story does not solve the perceived problem. If we step out of one story but the underlying emotional pattern is still active, it will create a lens that colors all that we see in our world, and over time, this emotional pattern will direct the creation of another story that does not serve us. In the final analysis, the story is merely a symptom. Therefore, when we treat the symptom, at best we find only temporary relief. This strategy never provides a long-term cure.

Bill had been attempting to deal with the stories running in his marriage and his professional career for over twenty years when I met him. Every attempt that he had made to shift his story or create a new one had resulted in only more of the same angry experiences. It was only when he began to deal with the underlying emotional patterning that he was able to address the root of his perceived problems and shift and change his life. Once the emotional patterning was aligned with aspects of love, Bill's life transformed.

Like Bill, we all have the potential for an emotional range that is far beyond what we are currently experiencing. There are boundaries to what we can know intellectually in this life, based on neurological constraints. There are limits to what we can achieve physically as well. However, when it comes to the emotions, our possible emotional range and the emotional depth that we can experience have unlimited potential.

By accessing dormant emotions and creating new emotional patterns that better serve us, we make possible the creation of a new life.

Once we start to evolve our emotions, there is no end to who we can become and what we can accomplish. Although we learned most of our emotional patterns at a young age, we can develop emotional range and depth at any time in our lives with the appropriate training. The relationship we have with our emotions has a direct bearing on our ability to create the vibrant lives we all deserve.

CHAPTER 5

The Power of Love and Fear

All emotions are pure which gather you and lift you up; that emotion is impure which seizes only one side of your being and so distorts you.

—RAINER MARIA RILKE

In any given moment, we are either aligned mentally and emotionally with fear or with love. We are constantly building our lives and creating our experience from one or the other. Love offers us the opportunity to consciously transform our lives and expand our states of being into new realms of possibility and experience. Fear struggles to maintain the status quo in our lives but ultimately results in a worsening of our situation.

When we are aligned with fear, we are in the realm of primal instinct. The part of the brain where fear is triggered is the amygdala. As a matter of survival, the amygdala is programmed to pay attention to what we fear. Most of us are afraid of painful emotions. They hurt. We don't have the tools to deal with them. Given that we are neurologically programmed to focus on what we are afraid of, when something arises in our environment that triggers our fear, we naturally focus on it. As a result, we run our fearful emotional patterns, thereby intensifying their neurological ruts.

Once fear triggers the amygdala, the amygdala triggers the reptilian brain to protect us from what we fear. The oldest and least evolved part of the human brain, the reptilian brain controls most animal and instinctive human behavior. It is in charge of the most basic functions of survival. The reptilian brain is where our *fight-or-flight instinct* lives. Fight-or-flight is a binary survival instinct. In other words, it is one or the other and there are no other options entertained. When we take action from this space of self-preservation, we do not think through our various options and weigh the odds. We just react.

The reptilian brain does not learn from mistakes. It does not have the capability of critical thinking or feeling emotions aligned with love. Its function is only to act in order to alleviate a threat in the moment. The reptilian brain is rigid, territorial, aggressive, paranoid, and obsessive. When the reptilian brain is activated, it has total priority over the rest of the brain, and it prevents adaptation and development. The reptilian brain is our defense system, and it does not negotiate.

When fearful emotions appear, the reptilian brain immediately looks for ways to alleviate the emotions through either fight or fight. As a result, we seek to either annihilate or avoid what we fear. This fight-or-flight response creates emotional coping mechanisms that are not in alignment with developing a healthy relationship with our emotions or the people in our lives. Although sitting with our emotions and allowing them to pass is an extremely beneficial exercise, the reptilian brain is not programmed to sit with what it fears, to allow the fearful emotion to express or to embrace it and transform it into something different. It does in the moment whatever it can to alleviate what it perceives as a threat.

When we are aligned with fearful emotions such as guilt, shame, sadness, unworthiness, anger, rage, betrayal, and humiliation, we lack the neurological ability to access our highest levels of intelligence and critical thinking. When we are in a state of fear, we only see our circumstances through the filters of the amygdala and the reptilian brain. As a result, we cannot see clearly what is actually in front of us. When we begin to step out of fear and align ourselves with love, we engage the most evolved portion of our brain, the prefrontal cortex, which gives us access to states of peace, love, and joy.

The amygdala and the reptilian brain direct most of the coping mechanisms we use on a regular basis to deal with fearful emotional patterns. Given that these portions of the brain are charged with survival and maintaining the status quo, it is impossible for us to transform and shift the circumstances of our lives at this level. When we engage these coping mechanisms over and over again, we are only strengthening the less-evolved portions of our brain. When operating from a state of fear, we only have access to strategies for coping in the moment—as opposed to accessing strategies that will allow us to prosper. The point of living is not to survive but instead to thrive. If we wish to consciously transform, we must become aware of the coping mechanisms that fear is sustaining and find the courage to live without them.

As a culture, we have decided that it is not okay to feel bad. Somewhere along the way, our society determined that we should always feel happy. If someone is feeling a painful emotion, we ask what is "wrong." The fact of the matter is: there is nothing wrong with feeling emotional discomfort. Feeling whatever you are feeling, without engaging in a myriad of unhealthy strategies for avoiding or severing yourself from the emotion, is actually a hallmark of the highly functional individual. Somewhere along the way, we have lost this concept.

Most of us were taught as children that certain emotions are "bad." Given that emotion is biologically wired into our brains, it makes no sense to criticize what is natural in our being. Despite this fact, boys are frequently told that it is wrong to cry and that they need to toughen up. After all, only "sissies" cry. Girls routinely have their youthful enthusiasm crushed by well-meaning parents who, in the face of spontaneous expressions of joy, tell their daughters to lower their voices. After all, ladies do not make a scene.

As children, many of us received the message that it was wrong to feel and express certain emotions. When we did express these emotions, there was often a painful consequence through either spanking or shaming. In such situations, we experienced different aspects of fear. Certain emotional expressions became dangerous, because at some point in our lives they became associated with increased emotional or physical pain. As a result, many of us adopted coping mechanisms that allowed us to distract ourselves from experiencing painful emotions.

Numbing ourselves and intellectualizing our emotions are two common coping mechanisms that almost everyone has used at some point in their lives. When we engage these coping methods for dealing with emotion, we cause ourselves serious mental, emotional, and physical difficulties. These difficulties are completely avoidable because emotions are merely a signal communicating that there is something within our inner matrix or external environment that is out of alignment. Emotion, like a fever, is a warning sign that we need to care for ourselves before the situation becomes life-threatening.

In our society, one of the most common coping mechanisms for dealing with emotion has become numbing ourselves through various methods of medication. When we feel overwhelmed by our emotions, it has become common to turn to alcohol, pharmaceuticals, or illegal drugs. However, medicating any emotion does nothing to address the underlying issue. Instead, the emotional pattern intensifies. Any foreign substance we put into the brain makes emotional balance increasingly difficult to achieve. As a result, the body is prevented from establishing a harmonious equilibrium.

During the last two decades, through an onslaught of television advertising, the pharmaceutical industry has marshaled this powerful force to peddle the message that there is something wrong with you when you feel negative emotions. This message plays into the communication that many of us received as children that some emotions are bad and that feeling them indicates that there is something wrong with us.

Antidepressants, sleeping pills, ADHD drugs, and anti-anxiety medications have been extremely profitable for the pharmaceutical industry. In recent years, the market for these drugs has exploded. What has helped to expand these markets are advertisements that seek to convince us that when we experience a normal range of human expression such as sadness or anxiety, or when we encounter sleepless nights and energetic kids, we need medication.

Television advertisements for prescription medications all seem to follow a typical format. The television screen is dark, usually gray. The person is alone and is obviously sad or tormented. What that person is experiencing is actually a normal range of human emotion. The voice narrating the advertisement then asks if you have ever experienced these same emotions. Because we all have experiences of sadness, we relate to the person on the screen. In addition, because of mirror neurons, when we watch the person in the advertisement experiencing these lower emotional states, we then experience the same depressed state as the person on the screen.

Next, the person in the advertisement pops a pill, and suddenly the sun is shining and that formerly sad or tormented person is now the life of the party. Now that person is laughing with friends and family or frolicking through a field of wheat and flowers. Most of us, at some point, have experienced the feeling of joy and connection in our lives. No matter what state we are in, all of us wish to feel better. As a result of our mirror neurons, we now experience these elevated emotional states watching the advertisement.

The advertisement is selling joy, love, and acceptance, not a chemical to help you avoid a perfectly normal emotion. As a result, for the average person who does not possess the skills and techniques to heal themselves emotionally, the pharmaceutical option has great appeal. Meanwhile, a voice that no one is listening to is describing the horrible side effects that can occur if you take this drug. Although you may no longer feel the emotional pain of someone leaving you, the advertisement warns that your liver may stop functioning.

One of my favorite examples is an advertisement for an "atypical antipsychotic" drug that was developed to treat schizophrenia and bipolar disorders. Recently this drug became approved for treating "major depression," and it is now widely marketed on television. However, what the advertisement shows is not a person suffering from a debilitating major-depressive episode, but instead something that resembles a normal state of melancholy.

In this advertisement, an attractive woman is looking out her glass door, standing across the room from her husband and teenage daughter. The scene is gray. The woman looks contemplative, perhaps a little sad, and rather lonely. The woman's voice announces that although she is taking an antidepressant, she feels like she could "use some more help." The narrator explains that "two out of three people who take antidepressants have unresolved symptoms" and suggests "talking to your doctor" about taking this drug or adding this drug on top of your current antidepressant.

In the next scene, the woman is outside with her family walking by a lake in the sunshine. Her husband holds her hand. Her teenage daughter puts her arm around her. The woman is now the smiling center of attention. Meanwhile, the narrator is listing the potential side effects from this extremely powerful psychotropic drug, including decreased white blood-cell count, increased blood-sugar levels, suicide, death, stroke, permanent involuntary repetitive movements, confusion, trouble swallowing, high fever, and coma. The message is clear: you should be willing to risk your life to make painful emotions disappear.

Statistics show just how effective these advertisements have been at convincing us that we need daily medication if we are experiencing negative emotions. The pharmaceutical companies now spend twice as much on advertising as they do on researching and developing drugs in the first place. Prescription drugs for depression, anxiety, ADHD, and sleeplessness are among the most highly advertised, with all four ranking in the top ten most widely prescribed medications. Antidepressant use has increased a staggering 400 percent since 1988. During 2008, over 164 million prescriptions were written for antidepressants, making them the third-most prescribed class of drugs in the United States. As of 2010, a stunning 25 percent of all women and 15 percent of all men in this country take medication for depression, anxiety, ADHD, or some other mental disorder.

Given that there is no evidence that we as a society suddenly became 400 percent more depressed, it is clear that the pharmaceutical industry has exploited and expanded our fear of emotional discomfort and turned it into a multibillion-dollar industry. Even if we are not among the numbers who are taking these types of pharmaceuticals, if we watch television, we have certainly been affected on some level by the multitude of these messages. When our televisions are on, there is virtually no way to avoid these commercials and the messages they carry into our homes.

The long-term impact of these drugs on the brain's functioning is not known, despite the fact that these drugs are now being prescribed to children as young as six years old. What we do know now is that the brain is not a static piece of machinery operating in the same way time after time. Instead, the brain is elastic and subject to change based on influence from environmental factors. Artificial, long-term alteration of the chemicals within the brain and the impact of this alteration on the mental, emotional, and physical bodies have not been studied—despite the fact that a large segment of our population is unwittingly part of an ongoing real-life experiment through their consumption of these pharmaceuticals. The situation amounts to nothing short of the legal doping of American society.

To make matters worse, studies conducted by Harvard University's placebo program under the direction of Dr. Irving Kirsch and highlighted on CBS's *60 Minutes* in February, 2012, show that for most people, antidepressants are only minimally more effective than a placebo. In Kirsch's studies, one of which utilized drug company data from clinical trials, those who were mildly to moderately depressed experienced no impact from taking antidepressants. Only those who were severely depressed experienced any clinically meaningful difference in their moods as a result of taking the medication. Studies at Brown University largely confirm Harvard's findings.

In other words, sugar pills are virtually as effective as the antidepressants that we are spending $11.6 billion on each year. And sugar pills contain none of the side effects. Dr. Kirsch's work studying the placebo showed that patients' brain function actually *changed* as a result of taking the placebo pill. In other words, he was able to show that the patients were not imagining the placebo effect. When patients experienced being cared for by a medical professional providing them with medication, their state of well-being actually shifted. As a result, in the Harvard studies, the placebo worked by feeding the connection between the mind, body, and emotions.

To add insult to injury, it is impossible for illegal drugs, alcohol, or even pharmaceuticals to cause emotional patterns to shift. Numbing is a seductive emotional strategy, because it gives us the impression that the emotions are less powerful. Of course, nothing could be further from the truth. The painful emotional patterns, which are hardwired into our brains, are still alive and thriving inside. The drug does nothing to impact the neurological patterns, but only momentarily interrupts our awareness of the painful emotion. It may feel like the *edge* to the emotion is taken off, but instead it is our *connection* to the emotion that is temporarily interrupted. As a result, our experience of the emotion is altered, but the underlying neurological pattern continues to run. When the drug wears off, the emotion is still there, as strong as it ever was, if not stronger. The feeling that there was less emotion was only an illusion.

Because most of us do not have effective strategies to deal with painful emotions, when an emotional crisis occurs, sometimes the only strategy that appears to be available is to take a pill or have a drink. In truth, the external events that appear as crises have not actually caused the emotion. The painful emotional pattern was already wired into our brains. *The external situation only triggered the pattern.* Because the emotional crisis is merely a symptom of the underlying emotional pattern, numbing ourselves to the symptom does nothing to address the root problem. As a result, neither the emotion nor our life changes.

* * *

A client of mine, Joel, first found his way to me following a difficult divorce. Joel was extremely sad and spending many of his days crying due to the loss of his wife. Although Joel was an intelligent professional working in a trust department at a large bank, he was inept at managing his emotions.

At first, Joel tried to think his way out of his emotions by intellectualizing them. Joel thought about why he was angry with his wife. Joel believed his wife had betrayed him. As a result, he felt worthless. Through the lens of his emotions, Joel could only see that his marriage was a failure because his wife did not love him anymore. Joel felt justified in feeling angry, sad, and worthless because of his wife's perceived betrayal. Joel told himself that he was entitled to feel this way, because he had lost what was most important in his life. After all, his wife had abandoned him.

Joel told himself that he could not be expected to feel anything but sadness in such a situation. As Joel continued to play these tapes in his mind, he found himself trapped in a compulsive cycle of thought and emotion that intensified every time he ran the neurological pattern. Over time, Joel became consumed by his powerful emotions.

Eventually, Joel's emotional pain reached the level where he could no longer effectively function at work or in his personal life. Because Joel lacked any strategies to effectively deal with the powerful emotions he was experiencing, in desperation, Joel turned to his doctor for help. Joel's doctor prescribed antidepressants to treat his emotional state.

The antidepressants were powerless to address Joel's hardwired emotional patterns, which had developed throughout his life and were the cause of the underlying problem. As the antidepressants failed to provide relief, Joel sought out other means to try to address the emotions that were surfacing in him. As a result, Joel began to do the work of Conscious Transformation. Through this work, Joel began to see that the strategies he had employed to try to address his painful emotions were actually exacerbating them.

Joel began to see that his emotional pain was not really caused by his wife or the divorce. Joel discovered that these patterns had actually lived inside of him almost his entire life. Through this work, he could see that these same emotional patterns had created many of the problems within his marriage to begin with. When challenging circumstances had arisen in the marriage, Joel had responded with the intelligence of these same emotional patterns of betrayal, sadness, anger, and unworthiness. Left unmanaged, these emotional patterns had wreaked havoc in his relationship and had led to divorce. Joel was finally able to see that he could no longer blame his wife for the emotions that dwelled within him.

As Joel began to tune into his inner matrix and sit with his emotions, he began to see that the circumstances of his life were not the cause of his feelings. Joel became aware that it was his emotional patterning that caused him to project through his mind a certain story for his life that supported experiencing his negative emotional patterns over and over again.

For example, when Joel would begin to think negatively about his wife, how she had left him, and how he had not been good enough for her, Joel was now aware that this story had little basis in reality. He could see that his mind was merely creating a situation to fuel the experience of his underlying patterns of sadness, unworthiness, and anger. He could also see that his emotions had created a lens through which he saw all situations in life. As a result, he had experienced sadness, anger, and unworthiness throughout his life in a multitude of different circumstances.

With this new awareness, Joel could stop his mind and place his attention on transforming the root of his suffering: his underlying emotional patterning. As he began to learn to separate his emotions from his mind, he could allow his emotions to express within without resistance. Joel could then apply the ninety-second rule, understanding that if he didn't allow his thoughts to feed his emotions then the emotion could only last for ninety seconds. As a result, he began to step into higher emotional states of being such as peace, gratitude, and love. He soon found that he no longer needed the antidepressants he had been taking.

Now when Joel thought about his wife, the emotional lens created by these new higher states significantly changed his story of their marriage. He was now grateful for the time he spent with his wife. He could see that their relationship served a powerful purpose in his life, and he also realized that she had not been the ultimate partner for him.

This new story opened up a space within him where he could now explore new relationships in a capacity that had not previously been possible. The change in Joel's underlying emotional patterning not only shifted his relationship with his former wife, but also transformed all of the relationships in his life. He was now able to engage in relationships in a space that had not previously existed for him. With his new emotional patterning of peace, gratitude, and love, Joel could now create dramatically different relationships, and as a result, his entire life changed.

Like Joel, we can all relate to a time in our lives when we faced a difficult situation. Whether that situation was a divorce, the end of a meaningful relationship, the death of a loved one, or the loss of a valued job, we found ourselves thinking the same negative thoughts and experiencing the same painful emotions over and over again. Driven by the emotions and fueled by the mind, our inner matrix created an unending circle of stronger and stronger emotional experiences from which we could not escape.

* * *

As we intellectualize emotion, the mind attempts to *think* its way out of an uncomfortable emotional experience. We analyze the emotion, uncover why we experience the emotion, and then try to think of a way not to experience the emotion any longer. Given that whatever we focus our energy on expands, this strategy is a complete failure. Far from alleviating the problem, trying to think ourselves out of an emotional rut only deepens the rut itself. It is completely counterproductive.

In the process of intellectualizing, we look for outside reasons for why we feel the way that we do. We blame our jobs, our spouses, our children, ourselves, or other things that present themselves in our environments. We believe that if we can only change our *outside* circumstances and get them to line up just right, then we can shift how we feel on the *inside*. Meanwhile, we are focusing on the emotion we wish to change and are unwittingly practicing how to feel that particular emotion. As a result, we experience more of that emotion, which leads to more thoughts about how to fix our world, which triggers more of the unwanted emotion, and on and on it goes.

For example, if we are angry at our spouse or significant other, we look for reasons why we feel the way we do. We may believe that we are angry because they are not spending enough time with us, they are taking us for granted, they are not pulling their weight financially, or they do not do their household chores. As we continue to think about why we are angry, instead of finding a solution for our anger, we become more and more angry, and the situation cycles in on itself. In the rare instance where one of these external situations does change, we find ourselves trying to figure out why we are still angry when what "made us angry" is no longer present. Until we see that our internal emotional state is what dictates all of our experience, we cannot begin to understand how the mind operates.

The most powerful force in our mind is not our thoughts but our emotions. Whatever emotion is present will drive the mind. The mind then creates thoughts to justify and validate the emotion. With the mind's support, the emotion is emboldened. In turn, the strengthened emotion again influences the mind, the thoughts show up to justify this emotional state, and the circle continues on and on. As the mind and emotions spiral together, the patterns in the inner matrix are reinforced, and they become harder and harder to change.

As the mind fuels the emotions, it creates reasons why we are justified and entitled to feel the ways we do. In this process, the mind gives the inner matrix permission for how we feel, so we can feel good about feeling bad. The typical pattern of justification is that something shows up and elicits a painful emotion in us. We then take action from this place of pain and give ourselves permission to hold on to the emotion. Because we blame our external circumstances for our emotions, we feel completely justified in our emotional experience and expression. It's not our fault that we are angry, sad, resentful, or rageful. Through justification, the inner matrix allows emotion full rein to wreak havoc in our lives and in the lives of those around us.

If someone betrays us, we can yell, scream, and seek out our revenge. After all, they deserve it. If someone is rude and insensitive to us, we can be rude and insensitive right back. Their behavior was outrageous. We feel justified, even entitled to engage these lower emotional patterns. Please remember, any time you hear the phrase "They deserved it," you can be sure that justification has reared its ugly little head.

Justification can even come in the veil of what might momentarily appear to be a positive emotion. If we are in a committed relationship and someone else comes along, this new "love" may justify our choice to leave our existing relationship. After all, our partner never appreciated us or treated us in the manner we deserved. We feel morally entitled to act on whatever emotion arises in response to our external world.

When the mind intellectualizes and justifies our feelings, we are conveniently never to blame for our harmful behavior. Accountability is out the window, no matter how much pain we inflict on others. Responsibility lies with the person "who started it" and "caused" us to behave in the way we did. As you can see, when we are in a place of justification, the focus is solely on what has shown up outside of us to trigger our emotions.

When we embrace this strategy, we give all our power away to whatever or whoever appears in our lives. We are completely at the mercy of others, who we see as responsible for our emotions. We may be angry, sad, jealous, or hateful, but only because of what another person did to us. We believe the other person or situation is responsible for how we feel and how we act. We have lost all power.

For examples that perfectly illustrate the process of emotional justification, all we have to do is turn on the radio. Pop music routinely tells the story of someone leaving, and as a result, the person who was left is forced to wallow in self-pity and depression, virtually unable to go on. Hip-hop loves to tell tales of someone being disrespected and then reacting with violence. However, perhaps the best example of a scene of emotional justification is found in the country song where the girl takes a baseball bat to her boyfriend's truck and destroys it because he has been unfaithful.

In a moment of complete righteousness, she exclaims that perhaps he will think twice before he cheats on his next girlfriend. The justification is clear. She has beaten her boyfriend's truck to a pulp, keyed its doors, and ripped up the interior out of a selfless concern that if she doesn't, he might emotionally wound his next girlfriend by cheating again. Now that is world-class justification!

Each one of these failed techniques for dealing with emotion is a type of unconscious reaction to our external world. As long as we are reacting to what is showing up in our world, we will never be free. We are not exercising free will if every time an emotion surfaces, we run the same patterned reaction over and over again. Emotional reaction is an enslavement supported by fear. We cannot be free and conscious adults until we learn how to master our emotions and take responsibility for them. Once we see clearly that emotions are just energy, there is no need to be controlled by or at the mercy of our emotions, we can begin to learn how to deal with them effectively.

Because lower emotions come with an experience of pain or discomfort, there is a natural tendency to want to get rid of that pain and discomfort by getting rid of the emotion. However, there is no way to get rid of what already exists inside of us. This is why all the strategies we have discussed so far fail.

Instead of attempting to get rid of painful emotions, we must reeducate our emotional body to function and operate at a higher capacity. If we cut our arm, we do not ignore it or amputate it. Instead, we attend to the wound and attempt to heal it. If there is an unhealthy emotion that appears in our emotional body, we must work with the emotional pattern to heal and transcend that state.

We heal the emotional body by training our inner matrix to function in higher states of emotional intelligence. As we move into these higher states, the emotional pain and discomfort we once experienced are eliminated. Because we create our lives from our emotional states, as we move into these higher states of being, the circumstances of our lives change and we attain the ability to create the lives we have envisioned.

When an undesirable or destructive emotion arises, we must train ourselves to stay with the emotion. We must allow the emotion to fully express itself inside of us in the present moment without resistance or reaction. Learning to stay present with our emotions and not feeling compelled to act upon them while giving them permission to fully express within us, is the key to shifting our emotional state and stepping out of the emotional prison.

Expressing the emotion in this context does not mean yelling, screaming, throwing something, punching a wall, hitting someone, saying something you will regret, or taking any other kind of external action. Instead, it means sitting still with our emotion and fully feeling and experiencing the emotion within ourselves without acting from that emotion. If we act out from our emotional state, we step back into and reinforce our old pattern, recreating the same painful experience in our lives that we are attempting to transcend. The key is to learn to stand still in the eye of the emotional storm, experience the feelings, and let the storm blow over.

The first step to transcending our emotional state is becoming sensitive to our feelings and being able to identify and acknowledge what emotion is actually present within us in any given situation. This skill of building sensitivity to how we feel is developed by tuning in several times throughout the day and asking ourselves, *In this moment, how do I feel?* Through this practice, we learn to identify the emotion that is present.

Once we can identify the emotional pattern that is active, we then can work with transcending that pattern. For example, if the pattern is anger—like Bill, who was angry with his employees—we must first be aware that we are feeling angry. It is then important to create a space where we can allow that anger to fully express itself within us, not fueling the anger with the mind but simply allowing it to unfold and dissipate.

Giving our emotion permission to express fully without feeding it through resistance or story allows us to take advantage of the ninety-second neurological lifespan of the emotion. Through this practice, we empower ourselves to step out of our old emotional ruts, experiencing and creating new emotional states. This is the practice of Conscious Transformation of our emotional patterns.

As we engage this practice, an interesting phenomenon occurs. When we allow an emotion aligned with fear such as anger, guilt, shame, or sadness to express fully without acting on it, the emotion tends to dissipate very quickly. On the other hand, when we engage the same practice aligned with the spectrum of love, such as peace, joy, compassion, and serenity, even when the state is not fueled by the mind, these states expand, becoming fuller and fuller. Underneath the static of the mental and emotional chatter, we discover who we are at our core. Our natural state is divine love, peace, and joy. As a result, when we tap into these higher states of being, they expand, unlike our temporary emotional states, which dissipate.

As we become sensitive to how we are feeling, we can use this phenomenon to our benefit by focusing on the emotional states that align us with love, causing those expressions to expand within us. When we align with the nature of fear, these states tend to constrict us, keeping us from the dreams and visions we wish to create. By aligning our emotions with aspects of love, these states expand within us, making our dreams and visions a reality.

As we sit with our emotions, we can acknowledge whether a particular emotion is aligning us with fear or love. We can begin to ask whether this emotional intelligence serves the vision we have for our life. We can also ask whether the emotion will serve to create the type of relationships we desire to experience. Once we can identify how we feel and what emotional patterns serve us in creating our visions, we have the ability to consciously choose which emotions to align with and take action from. Through this process, we can begin to actively create our lives. By engaging this conscious choice, we are accessing another level of Conscious Transformation.

Many wisdom traditions have long taught the importance of staying present in the moment. It is our emotional patterns that take us out of the present and into the experience of either our past or an unmanifested future. As a result, our emotional patterns recreate the same experiences over and over again in order to sustain their existence. The fear-based emotional patterns within will not lead us to becoming aware in the present moment; it's almost as if they have a stake in preventing it, for if we stay present and choose not to engage them, over time, they will cease to exist. Staying present in the moment takes practice, but remember: if you can stay present with an emotion without engaging a story around it and just breathe for ninety seconds, the emotion cannot sustain itself.

Staying present with a painful emotion does take practice. Most of us have been utilizing these unhealthy techniques for decades, so it may take some time for a healthy strategy of emotional management to become our default. As soon as we begin stepping into and taking action from these new emotional patterns, the impact on our relationships and in our lives is profound, elevating all aspects of our mental, emotional, and physical bodies. When we make the conscious decision to cultivate peace, compassion, joy, and divine love, all aspects of the inner matrix are transformed.

CHAPTER 6

Where You Live

Our bodies are our gardens, to which our wills are gardeners.

—WILLIAM SHAKESPEARE

The connection between emotion and the body is undeniable. When dealing with intense emotional states, we often get a stomachache. Stomach pain and ulcers are commonly related to stress and the inability to manage our emotions. When we are sad and depressed, the body becomes tired and fatigued. We have little energy for our daily activities and wish only to sleep.

When we become very angry, by contrast, our bodies are flooded with adrenaline. This causes our heart to race, our chest to tighten, our blood pressure to increase, and our digestive system to shut down. Our body temperature can even rise by as much as two or three degrees to 101 degrees Fahrenheit, which is considered a fever. Increased stress is placed on the liver and kidneys, which now must detoxify the adrenaline. All of these physical responses create additional stresses on the body. If we engage anger on a consistent basis, over time the body will break down, significantly decreasing our lifespan.

On the other hand, when we experience states of joy and excitement, we have plenty of energy. When we are in a state of peace, our physical body may experience deep states of relaxation. The body feels flexible and supple in response. Our pulse slows, and our chest may lighten. Our immune system is strengthened, and our ability to fight disease substantially increases. When we step into higher emotional states, we maintain a youthful vitality in the body and aging is slowed.

When we are overwhelmed by strong emotions and don't know what to do with them, it is common to suppress the emotions and hold them inside the body. We might feel ourselves *swallowing* the emotion, and experience the emotion living in the pit of our stomach. A common phrase used to describe this phenomenon is *stomaching* one's emotions. Stomaching emotion is the "fake it until you make it" approach to emotion. We may smile at the world, when we are on the verge of exploding. We try to put on an appropriate face while we stuff more and more of the emotion down deeper and deeper inside. We even describe uncomfortable situations as making our stomach hurt. As we continue to stomach more and more emotion, we feed the emotion, and the inner sensation of the emotion intensifies. This strategy is a physical way of trying to deal with emotion.

When we suppress our emotion, it continues to build until we cannot hold any more. The pressure becomes unbearable, and at some point, what we have stuffed down erupts like a volcano in an uncontrollable explosion, damaging our relationships and those around us. We do not have any choice over when this force is unleashed. Instead, we burst at the seams.

The emotional intensity expressed in that moment does not match the intensity of the situation in which it is being expressed. Our reaction is just not commensurate with the situation in which the reaction occurs. Those around us may be puzzled at why we are *suddenly* so emotional. It does not make any sense to them. To the outside world, it may appear that we are overreacting. Our reaction, of course, will be in direct proportion to what we have been stuffing down inside of us for an extended period of time.

A typical example of an emotion that we often stomach is anger. Because being an angry person is not socially desirable, particularly not for women, many of us swallow our anger and stomach it instead of expressing it. In our stomach, the anger festers and builds until it explodes with great intensity. When the explosion is over, we may feel a short-lived emotional release, but more often, the experience is followed by a realization that in the moment, we acted like a crazy person. We said or did things that were hurtful to another. We experience feelings of regret, shame, guilt, unworthiness, and even anger at ourselves for having behaved so badly. As a result, the cycle of stomaching our emotions begins all over again. Another layer is laid, the emotional pattern is deepened, and the walls of the prison extend even higher, taking a severe toll on our physical body.

If I asked you to hold your arm straight out from your body and not to lower it, you would not have a problem for the first few minutes. After ten or fifteen minutes, though, you would be in intense pain. The same is true with regard to suppressing emotion. Although it is no problem to deal with negative emotions in short bursts, if we experience intense emotional states for long periods of time, the body begins to break down. In today's stress-filled world, caring for the body is vitally important, in order to provide ourselves with tools to create balance and well-being inside, instead of creating additional stress.

To see how the physical body's state of well-being impacts both the mind and the emotions, consider how we feel when we have the flu. In this state, it is difficult to think clearly or to be joyful. Like children, when we become tired we have a greater tendency to regress into undesirable emotional states. We often become cranky and irritable. When we are well-rested and vibrant, it is easier to connect to states of peace and joy.

The reverse is also true: our mental state affects our physical condition. When our minds are busy thinking of the multitude of tasks that we need to accomplish at work today, our bodies will feel tense and even tired. When we are mentally stressed, our muscles often ache and we may feel physically weak. On the other hand, when we sit to meditate and still our minds, our bodies automatically relax.

The scientific community is increasingly recognizing the connection between stress and illness. A Harvard University study estimates that at least sixty to ninety percent of all doctor visits are stress-related. The Centers for Disease Control and Prevention similarly estimates that up to ninety percent of doctor visits are triggered by a stress-related illness. Nearly fifty percent of Americans report that they regularly lie awake at night because of stress. Research published by the *Journal of the American Medical Association* has concluded that stress is as bad for your heart as smoking and high cholesterol and has confirmed the link between stress and increased risk for heart attacks, depression, and cancer. Science has established that stress also lowers our immune response. When we are stressed, our body's mechanism for fighting disease is severely compromised and we become vulnerable to a variety of illnesses.

It is important to note that the impact of stress on the immune system can last long after the stressful event is over. For example, studies have shown that even years after enduring a stressful emotional situation, such as caring for a patient with Alzheimer's, we remain more susceptible to disease due to this past stress. Western medicine is now proving what Eastern medicine has taught for thousands of years: at the root of every disease is an emotional imbalance.

As we previously discussed, our bodies are programmed to guard against external threats as a survival mechanism. When we perceive a threat, the fear we experience activates our fight-or-flight system. The fight-or-flight system automatically drains energy away from critical bodily functions such as digestion and immune function in order to funnel that energy to the adrenals.

When human beings lived in more primitive cultures, it was critical that they be able to escape from common physical threats. When a wild animal was attacking, the body simply could not be bothered with whether digestion and immune function were at optimal levels. Instead, it was necessary that high levels of adrenaline be produced in our bodies to enable us to either run away from or fight off the wild beast. Without this fight-or-flight system to escape threats, there would be no body left for digestion or immune function to occur within. As a result, it was critical that the fight-or-flight system take precedence over all other bodily functions.

In our modern society, however, we encounter very few external threats to our physical existence. It is rare that we run into a wild animal that wishes to rip us to shreds. However, when we live in fear-based emotional states, we view our circumstances through the lens of our fearful patterns. As a result, our mind perceives threats around every corner that do not even exist. For example, if we are in a state of continual anxiety, our emotions drive the mind to see even the most benign circumstances as threatening. The fear we experience activates our adrenal system and drains energy from our digestion and immune systems and other critical bodily functions. Because everything looks like a threat when we hold fear-based emotional patterns, we find ourselves in a constant state of high alert.

Today our own internal fear-based emotional patterns now pose the greatest threat to our physical health and well-being. The system that was constructed to protect our physical bodies from external threats now threatens our well-being because of our fear. Our bodies simply were not designed to distinguish between generalized anxiety about a difficult boss at work and the tiger that wants to kill us. Because our fear-based emotional patterns are triggered by whatever shows up in our environment, we are in a continual state of stress that degrades our bodies and cripples our immune function. In the end, our fearful emotional patterning damages our physical body by trying to avoid a threat that never existed in the first place.

Few people recognize the connection between stress and emotion. Stress is fear-based emotion. The stronger and more intense the fear-based emotion is, the greater its negative impact on our physical body. When we experience emotions that align with a state of love, such as joy, peace, and tranquility, we do not experience a state of stress, and our body is not negatively impacted. Just because we experience intense periods in our lives does not mean that we have to endure stress—if we have mastered our emotional patterns. It is possible to live a very active and full lifestyle while still maintaining optimal health, if we are not enduring the negative emotional patterning that stresses our physicality.

Most of us have seen a connection between stress in our own lives and physical illness. From time to time, after a particularly stressful period, many of us have noticed that we tend to get sick. In addition to reducing our ability to fight disease, stress actually triggers it. For example, lysogenic viruses are viruses that lie dormant in our cells until an event causes the virus to become active. Stress is one such event that causes viruses to enter a stage where the cells they have infected rupture and our bodies become infected. The combination of lysogenic triggers and lowered immune response, both caused by our stress levels, is one explanation for this common phenomenon.

Due to the pace of our modern world and the increased levels of intensity that we endure, a practice of Conscious Transformation is as essential to our health and well-being as diet and exercise. If we do not have an internal discipline or practice of developing our inner matrix at the level of our mind, body, emotion, and spirit, we are at a great deficit and will not function optimally.

In a world of cell phones, email, text messaging, and other forms of constant communication, we are now expected to be available 24/7. Given that we cannot make the modern world slow down, it is essential that we develop the skills necessary to thrive in it. Even twenty years ago, a person might be able to survive without knowing these techniques, but today, in a time of instant accessibility and distraction, we encounter unparalleled levels of emotional and mental stress. The serious toll this takes on the physical body cannot be ignored.

As a result of the constant demands on our time and attention, many of us have lost our connection with our own internal lives. Tools to achieve and enhance this connection, such as silence and personal introspection, have faded from our societal landscape. Inner connection and an awareness of our inner matrix are critical components for healthy, vibrant lives.

The body also has significant influence on the mind and the emotions. When we tend to our bodies, along with our mental, emotional, and spiritual selves, we accelerate our process of Conscious Transformation and step onto the path toward optimal health and well-being. As the great Buddha once said, "To keep the body in good health is a duty ... otherwise we shall not be able to keep our mind strong and clear."

The body actually has its own highly refined communication system that tells us how to keep the body in good health, if we merely learn to listen to it. As we have previously discussed, the mind and the emotions both have a language of their own. The body also has a language that tells us what serves and what injures our well-being. If we think about animals in the wild, they instinctively understand when something will harm them. Through instinct and intuition, an animal can walk up to a poisonous food and then turn and walk away from it, knowing it does not serve. We actually possess the same system.

Unfortunately, in our modern society, many of us are numb to our body's own communication system, or we choose to ignore it. Sometimes we miss our body's communications because we are distracted by the busyness of our existence. In order to achieve optimum health, we must reconnect to our body's communications and become sensitive to what serves and does not serve our bodies.

We can think of our body's communication system as a giant radar dish that both takes in and sends out information. When our body wishes to communicate about something in the environment, it sends out a signal via sensation. For example, the body may send the signal that it needs rest by indicating that it feels tired. If we are in tune with our body and understand what it is trying to communicate, then we would ask what was causing our fatigue. Do we need more sleep? Have we been eating healthy foods? Are we emotionally or mentally exhausted? What shifts can we make or action can we take to restore vibrancy to our physical body? We must approach communication with our body with this type of analysis and introspection if we are to maximize our physical well-being.

Unfortunately, instead of asking ourselves what the underlying cause is for such a communication, we often respond by looking for a quick fix to numb the body's message. For example, when we feel fatigue, we might pound an energy drink or order a latte with a double shot of espresso. This fix allows us to momentarily get past the sensation of discomfort and push ourselves even harder, which is the opposite of what the body is requesting. Although the original communication of discomfort from our body is subtle and quiet, if ignored in the long term, the murmurs become deafening screams of illness and disease.

When we fail to heed our body's warnings that we are fatigued and tired, we make stupid mistakes and cannot operate optimally. Our performance at work suffers, and we forget details that normally would not escape our attention. We may have an accident and injure ourselves. On an emotional level, we become more irritable and easily triggered. In situations where we would normally have patience with our children or a loved one, we suddenly lose our temper.

When we suffer back pain, instead of addressing the weakness or injury our body is communicating, we often ignore it, going about our daily lives without addressing the underlying cause. When the pain increases over time, we may take a pill to eliminate the pain, but we continue about our normal routine without doing anything to address the weakness or injury being communicated. We do not do exercises to strengthen the back. We do not engage a stretching regime to increase our flexibility. One day, our back goes out, and we are told that we need surgery.

When we have a headache, we typically reach for a painkiller instead of taking the time to ask why it is that we have a headache in the first place. Are we lacking protein? Could we be dehydrated? Perhaps we are allergic to something we are eating. Do we have a fear-based emotional pattern that is causing us to experience stress?

All of us have had the experience of realizing that we are coming down with something but not doing anything about it. We tell ourselves that we are too busy. After all, it is only a little cold. We ignore the symptoms, and ultimately it turns into an infection that is more serious. If we had heeded our body's early communications, we could have taken action, such as getting a little extra sleep to help the body fight the virus.

The fact of the matter is that most serious illnesses are preceded by a myriad of communications from our bodies. We might notice something out of the norm for our body. Pain or discomfort might appear. We just don't feel right. Because the symptoms are not extreme, we ignore the communication. It is oftentimes not until we are unable to function in our lives, because we can no longer go to work or take care of the kids, that we finally attend to the issue at hand. Then we listen and tend to the situation only because our capacity has been diminished. At this point, it might seem too late to heal the body. At a minimum, it takes much more to heal the body than it would have if the symptoms had been addressed when they originally arose.

What is critical to understand is that pain is a method of communication from our bodies. It is not an irritant that should be ignored. It is not an inconvenience to be overcome. It is not a symptom that needs to be masked. Instead, it is a sign of an issue that needs to be addressed.

On a path of Conscious Transformation, we begin to step out of the modern Western ideology of only caring for the body when it is sick. Instead, we begin to embrace a holistic approach to health that focuses on maintaining the body's vibrancy. The goal is to maintain a state of wellness and ensure that the body does not break down in the first place.

In Eastern medicine, the emphasis has long been geared toward keeping individuals healthy as opposed to just healing them when they are sick. In ancient times, villages had a healer whose job it was to ensure that villagers stayed healthy. If people in the village became ill, it did not bode well for the healer. Today, our health care system is built on a model where professionals are paid when their patients are sick instead of being compensated to keep them well. It is critical that we begin to shift our focus to wellness.

However, even in situations where we are already experiencing illness or disease, it is not too late to shift and bring the body into a healthy state of being. Medical literature is full of stories where a patient walks into a doctor's office and is told that he or she either has an incurable medical condition or very little time to live. The patient defies the odds and recovers.

We classify such situations as miracles or scientific anomalies. In actuality, these situations are neither. What happens in such a case is that the body moves into its natural state of being. The person rejects the diagnosis and instead shifts and changes from the state of illness into a state of physical, mental, emotional, and spiritual vibrancy that supports profound healing at a deep level.

* * *

A client of mine, Diane, was diagnosed with a genetic defect in her blood's natural clotting mechanism the year she turned thirty. She discovered this situation when she woke up one morning and found the right side of her body completely numb. She had suffered a small stroke known as a transient ischemic attack or TIA. A month later, she suffered a second stroke. Diane was a busy professional who had ignored the dizziness she had been experiencing for months.

Diane's hematologist determined that she had a genetic defect causing her body to produce only about 60 percent of the needed levels of antithrombin III. Antithrombin III is one of the body's natural substances that breaks down clots in the bloodstream. Diane was told that there was no cure for her condition. She was also told there was no hope that there ever would be a cure, because the condition she had was so rare that no pharmaceutical company would ever spend the money to find a solution.

In order to prevent further strokes, Diane's doctors turned her into a hemophiliac by putting her on high doses of blood thinners whose chemical composition was akin to rat poison. As a result, Diane, who had lived a very active life, could no longer go hiking, horseback riding, snow skiing, water skiing, or even bicycle riding due to the risk that if she suffered a fall, she would undoubtedly bleed to death. Given the danger of stroke from her underlying illness or bleed from her treatment, Diane was told that her lifespan would be significantly limited. The doctors believed that either a stroke or bleed would ultimately kill her.

For over a decade, Diane struggled to control her blood levels, going from one life-threatening situation to the next. Diane's body did not adapt well to the blood thinners and her blood levels would swing from dangerously thin to life threateningly thick. When her blood would become too thick, she would throw a clot to the brain, eye, or lung with frightening consequences. She found herself unable to breathe in a movie theater one time, because of a pulmonary embolism and was rushed to the emergency room. During a hearing in court one day, she threw a clot to her eye and lost sight in that eye for almost twenty-four hours.

When her blood would also become too thin, she suffer internal bleeding into parts of her body. When, contrary to her doctor's orders she gave birth to a baby girl, Diane developed complications and almost bled to death. She experienced routine bleeds causing severe damage to her right knee. After the first such bleed, she found herself in physical therapy for almost eight months. On numerous occasions, she bled into her elbow and back, experiencing such severe pain that she spent hours on end in emergency rooms and was even hospitalized.

Diane was married with two small daughters. Her greatest fear was that she would never live to see her daughters grow up. About six months after she started working with me privately and doing a daily meditation program that I created for her, her symptoms went away. Diane no longer bled into her joints. Her body no longer threw dangerous clots. The routine trips to the emergency room ceased. For the first time in years, Diane seemed to be healthy.

Four years later, Diane contracted influenza and found herself back in her hematologist's office. Because she had become infected as a result of the flu, she required an antibiotic to heal. In the past, antibiotics had interacted negatively with Diane's blood thinners and had caused wild swings in her blood levels, which had put her life at risk from internal bleeding. This time, as her hematologist monitored her condition, her blood levels remained stable despite the fact that she was taking a potent antibiotic.

The hematologist asked Diane what doctor had been monitoring her over the last four years. When my client informed her doctor that no one had been monitoring her, at first he did not believe her. When my client insisted that she had not had any problems for four years, her doctor responded that such an outcome was "impossible." He told her that he had used her as a case study for her rare illness. She joked with him that he would need to stop that now that she was healthy. The hematologist was shocked.

A year after this visit to her hematologist, Diane got up the courage to have her blood levels retested to determine whether she still had the genetic issue that had plagued her for seventeen years. Diane believed that her work with me had caused her damaged gene to begin functioning in the way it was intended, although there were no studies regarding her particular illness, and mainstream hematology believed that such an outcome was impossible. Diane's doctor had explained to her that antithrombin III, the protein that she lacked, reached its permanent level by the time a person turned two years of age and did not vary after that point.

Despite this fact, Diane persisted with retesting. The results were stunning. Her antithrombin III levels had doubled since her first stroke. Diane's doctor ordered another round of testing to make certain there was not a mistake with the lab. When the tests came back in normal range for a second time, my client was able to go off of her blood thinners and assume a normal life for the first time in seventeen years. Two days after she received her results, she threw away her blood thinners, bought a bicycle, and went on her first bicycle ride ever with her two young daughters.

Although at first blush, it may seem unlikely that such an outcome could be tied to meditation, there is now a wealth of scientific support for our ability to turn on and off certain genes in our bodies. The emerging science of epigenetics is the study of our biologic responses to environmental stressors. The epigenome sits on top of our genes and acts as a type of *dimmer switch* that can change a gene's intensity of expression. Our environment directs these genetic switches. The epigenome can turn a gene on, turn a gene off, make the gene loud, or reduce the gene to a mere whisper. These patterns of gene expression are then passed on to the next generation.

This emerging body of science proves the amazing power that factors such as diet and stress have on our bodies. For example, studies have shown that women who eat poorly during their pregnancy have children who are at a significantly higher risk for cardiovascular disease. In 2009, the United States' National Institutes of Health allotted $190 million toward epigenetic research. It is now believed that only 2 percent of our genes are actually fixed in their expression. In other words, we can turn the other 98 percent off and on—or alter how they are expressed—by the choices we make in this lifetime. This may be the most empowering news of the new millennium.

Although most of the epigenetic research to date focuses on understanding what environmental factors trigger disease, studies are now beginning to look at what environmental factors can trigger health through this epigenetic process. Diet, exercise, and meditation are the three factors that have been identified as having a positive epigenetic impact.

A 2008 study conducted by Dr. Herbert Benson's group at Harvard University took blood samples from a group of individuals who had routinely meditated over a number of years and corresponding samples from a group who had never meditated. Dr. Benson found that the long-term meditators had over one thousand genes turned *on* for disease prevention and *off* for disease causation, which was statistically significant for the meditators' group.

Dr. Benson then taught the group that had never meditated a ten-minute daily meditation regime that they executed for six weeks. At the end of this period, these new meditators had changed their genetic expression by turning on and off hundreds of the genes that had been identified in the long-term meditators for disease prevention and causation. Science has now shown that certain meditation practices are powerful tools to shift and change our physical health as well as our mental and emotional states. It is possible to find studies on the positive impact of meditation on almost every major disease.

Just as thoughts create the condition of our mind and our feelings create the condition of our emotions, nutrition and exercise are primarily responsible for creating the condition of the physical body. This should not be news. The founder of modern Western medicine, the Ancient Greek physician Hippocrates, for whom the physician's Hippocratic Oath is named, stated, "Let food be thy medicine."

The food that we consume not only contains essential nutrients, but it also embodies essential life force and energy necessary to support our physical bodies. After all, food is energy. The vibratory intelligence in the food we eat fuels, nourishes, and actually *becomes* our physical bodies, influencing our own level of consciousness. As a result, our mental, emotional, physical, and spiritual states are all affected by the food we consume. The old saying "You are what you eat" is all too true.

There was a time when most of our food came from living, whole foods, eaten straight off of the vine. Today, that is not the case. As soon as food is harvested, it begins to die. A tomato picked from the vine will only live for a few days. Both the nutritional value and the life force in the food begin to deteriorate once the food is harvested. Today, much of our conventional food source is shipped to our grocery stores from halfway around the world.

Our attitude with regard to food has shifted as well. Instead of eating to live, many in our society now live to eat. Food has become entertainment and comfort as opposed to medicine, as we have stepped away from listening to the communications from our bodies about what serves and what does not. Most of us are so detached from our bodies' communication systems that we do not even realize when we are engaging in behavior that is killing us.

Unlike the deer in nature that intuitively knows when food is poisonous and shies away from eating it, most people eat food that is damaging their bodies without any awareness of the harm it is causing. Like smoking, eating unhealthy food brings about a slow and almost certain death. The evidence to support this state of physical disconnection can be found by looking at the current condition of humanity's overall physical health.

The physical condition of many people's bodies exemplifies just how far we have strayed from Hippocrates's prescription. Cancer, diabetes, obesity, and heart issues affect more individuals with every passing day. One in every three children born in the United States during the year 2000 will develop diabetes in their lifetime. Diabetes will cut an average of seventeen to twenty years from an individual's lifespan.

The World Health Organization has declared obesity a global epidemic, noting that obesity rates have doubled in every region of the world between 1980 and 2008. Sixty percent of Americans are overweight. Over one-third of the people in the United States, or seventy-three million people, are obese. Skyrocketing childhood obesity levels virtually guarantee that adult obesity rates will continue to increase.

Medical professionals estimate that obesity takes an average of twelve years from an individual's lifespan. Obesity has been linked to a staggering list of illnesses, including hypertension, coronary heart disease, adult-onset diabetes, stroke, gall bladder disease, osteoarthritis, sleep apnea, respiratory problems, endometrial cancer, breast cancer, prostate cancer, colon cancers, high cholesterol, types of hepatitis, insulin resistance, breathlessness, asthma, reproductive hormone abnormalities, polycystic ovarian syndrome, impaired fertility, and lower back pain.

But why are so many people now obese? Long gone are the days where the local family farmer controlled our food supply. Today, many of the seeds from which our food is grown are not the same seeds that produced our crops even two decades ago. Hybridization and genetic alteration of our food supply has resulted in vastly different and yet mostly untested sources of nutrition. The seeds that produced the food that we once ate had been around for thousands of years. To alter nature's genetic code and believe that it will not have a deleterious impact on our health flies in the face of basic common sense.

Genetically modified foods, referred to as GMOs, are increasingly prevalent on our food shelves. Foods that have been genetically modified do not contain any warning to the consumer that they have been altered. GMOs have not been subject to testing to determine whether they are safe for human consumption. Seventy-five percent of foods now contain at least some ingredient that has been genetically modified. Although increasingly popular in the United States, Europe began to ban GMOs over a decade ago due to health concerns, and government bans on them have continued to spread worldwide.

One of the reasons that corporations have genetically modified our food supply is to invent crops that can withstand the use of greater amounts of insecticides, fertilizers, and pesticides. For example, chemical companies have invented variations of seeds that tolerate vastly increased amounts of herbicide without killing the plant. These insecticides, fertilizers, pesticides, and other chemicals have poisoned our conventional food supply.

It has been known for decades that even short-term exposure to certain amounts of these chemicals kills people. The United Nations reports that thousands of adults and children, primarily in underdeveloped countries, die every year from pesticide poisoning. These chemicals have contributed to the decrease in our water quality, which has also been severely compromised by a variety of pollution sources and other environmental factors.

A 2012 joint study between researchers at the University of Texas and Washington State University, published in the *Proceedings of the National Academy of Science*, researched the genetic implications of generational exposure of rats to a common fungicide. The study found that the fungicide damaged brain development and function, causing the third generation of rats to be less able to deal with stress and anxiety. The study concludes that increases in disorders such as autism and bipolar disorder may be connected to such exposure over time.

One of the major food sources in the United States containing processed foods laden with pesticides and other chemical additives is *fast food*. United States Surgeon General David Satcher stated, "Fast food is a major contributor to the obesity epidemic." Despite these facts, each day, one in every four Americans visits a fast-food restaurant, and every day, McDonald's alone feeds more than forty-six million people, which is more than the population of Spain.

Ingesting fast food comes with serious health risks. Eating fast food has been shown to double your risk of insulin resistance, which is a precursor to diabetes. In addition to its link to obesity, food quality, content, and processing at fast-food chains causes severe health risks. As McDonald's spokesperson admitted in the documentary *Super Size Me,* "Any processing our foods undergo make them more dangerous than unprocessed foods."

Processed foods have also been linked to cancer. In a University of Hawaii study spanning seven years and involving more than 200,000 individuals, those who ate the most processed meats had a 67 percent higher risk of pancreatic cancer than those who ate little or no processed meat products.

Research published in the *Journal of Cancer Epidemiology* further found that refined carbohydrates such as white flour, sugar, and high fructose corn syrup are also linked to cancer. This study of more than 1,000 women found that those who received 57 percent or more of their total caloric intake from refined carbohydrates had a 220 percent higher risk of breast cancer than women eating more-balanced diets.

The primary reason we are consuming large quantities of unhealthy food is that we were programmed and educated at an early age to accept this level of nutrition. Just as we receive mental and emotional patterning, the way we take care of our physical being and nourish our body was established at an early age. As a result, we cannot see that certain kinds of food basically poison our bodies. Studies show that most children can recognize the McDonald's arches before they can speak. Many parents use fast food as a treat for their children. Most of us have a fond memory of eating our favorite fast food as a child, which then linked fast food to a positive emotional experience.

Another reason we desire these foods is that we actually acquire a physiological addiction to high-fat and high-sugar foods. Ingestion of high-fat and high-sugar foods has been shown to alter hormones and the functioning of the brain's hypothalamus, creating addictions in the brain. These addictions lead to craving higher and higher quantities of such foods—hence we are being *super sized.*

Without high-quality food, we cannot expect high-quality performance from our mental, emotional, physical, and spiritual aspects. For example, I happen to enjoy fast cars, and as a result, I own one. If I put 87 octane gasoline in my car, which is of low quality, my engine knocks, pings, and does not run in the way it was built to perform. On the other hand, if I feed it a high-octane fuel, it has impressive power.

Although the early symptoms of using low-quality fuel may not be dramatic, over time, if I continue feeding my car marginal fuel, the engine will gum up, and more serious problems will arise. The same is true for our bodies. Although we can get by in the short-term eating processed, conventional food without noticing ill side-effects, over time, the body will break down. It will cease to function at its optimal capacity, and serious health problems will arise.

As professional athletes know, if they wish to be at the top of their game, they cannot eat an unhealthy diet and expect to perform optimally. Instead, they must spend a significant amount of time focused on their nutrition. Although we may not be professional athletes, nutrition is an essential component if we wish to perform at optimal levels in our professional lives and personal relationships.

One reason that physical health does not always rise to the level of a top priority is that most people fail to make the connection between the food they are eating and the emotional and mental states they are experiencing. Although not everyone may aspire to be in top physical form, everyone wishes to feel good in the body.

The physical patterning that determines the food we eat has a direct relationship with how we feel emotionally. As most parents learn early on, keeping a child's blood sugar relatively level is important for family harmony. When children become hungry, they become cranky and their emotional state quickly deteriorates. When they are fed large quantities of sugar, they bounce off the walls for a short period of time, only to crash in what is often an emotional fit.

Although the impact of poor food consumption can be subtler in adults, the chemistry is the same no matter the age. When we consume foods that are high in sugar, we initially feel good, but that momentary high is soon followed by fatigue, depression, and lethargy. On the other hand, when we eat fresh, organic produce, we will naturally have higher levels of energy and vitality while making it easier to sustain an emotional state that is more balanced. Our mental state is affected by the food we eat as well. Sugary foods cause us to have a foggy mind, making it difficult to think. A diet rich in organic produce supports clarity of thought and optimal brain function.

In order to establish a healthy relationship with food, we must stop putting what amounts to 87 percent octane in our bodies. It is critical that we become aware of what we are eating and consciously choose healthy food in order to break our destructive eating patterns. We must educate ourselves about our food so that we can use our diet to raise instead of lower our level of consciousness.

As we begin the practice of conscious eating, we must begin to connect with and train our body's communication systems. Meditation can put us back in touch with our body's innate ability to communicate to us what is and is not healthy. Every time we eat, our body sends a communiqué in response to what we are giving it. Most of us have just become insensitive to the messages we are receiving.

Because so many of us have numbed our communication systems over time, in order to clearly hear the body, we must practice this skill on a daily basis and reconnect to the body's language. If we focus on tuning in to it and what it is trying to tell us, its voice will resurface in a relatively short period of time. When we become sensitive to what our body is telling us, we can begin to navigate our food choices in a way that will create optimal health and well-being. Meditation can create that renewed sensitivity for us.

Take a moment now and tune in to your body. Become aware of what sensations your body is feeling. Is the body hot or cold? Is it tense or relaxed? Is the body fatigued or energized? Now take a moment and imagine a fast-food meal with your physical senses. Think of how it smells. Think of how it tastes. Think of the way it feels as you envision yourself putting this meal into your mouth, chewing it, and swallowing it. Now be aware of how your body reacts. For me, when I even think of fast food, my stomach begins to ache, and I feel mildly nauseated. My body has no problem communicating that this food does not serve my highest state of well-being.

Once again, take a moment to tune in to your body and become aware of what sensations you feel. Now picture yourself choosing a piece of healthy organic produce, perhaps your favorite type of apple or a piece of well-prepared locally raised organic beef or even an all-natural fruit smoothie. Notice the texture, the smell, the color, and the sound if it has one. Now be aware of how your body reacts as you put it into your mouth and start chewing it, tasting the flavors as they fill your mouth.

When I think of eating my favorite organic apple, I feel a sense of energy well up inside and a tingling sensation throughout my body. This experience is in sharp contrast to my experience with fast food.

When tuning in to something that is going to be of benefit, we have an experience of an opening or a wanting. With regard to what is not healthy or does not serve, there is a sense of contraction or rejection. As you tuned in to fast food and organic produce, were you able to tell the differences in the sensations that showed up in your body?

Knowing it is destructive for their bodies, some who tune in to the fast-food meal will still experience a craving or pleasurable sensation. This is a communication from the unhealthy pattern supporting a low vibration of consciousness within the body. This craving is the same as someone who is addicted to an unhealthy substance such as cigarettes, alcohol, or cocaine. If we have an unhealthy pattern of eating, then at first, this is the only communication we will be able to access. The body will simply not know how to move us toward healthy choices. This is the reason why most diets fail. Until we shift and change the unhealthy patterns, ultimately, we will revert back to them.

Just as emotions drive the patterns of thought in our minds, emotion is also the driving force behind our eating patterns. For most of us, food has become an emotional event as opposed to a mindful exercise to support and sustain the body. We eat from a place inside of us that desires entertainment, distraction, or comfort, as opposed to eating to nourish and care for our bodies. When we are sad, we reach for the carton of ice cream to comfort and soothe us. A bout of momentary anxiety sends us straight for a sugary snack. We feel lonely or disappointed and crave a starchy meal.

Over time, we tie eating certain unhealthy foods to certain lower emotional states. We even refer to such foods as *comfort foods*. Of course, these foods do nothing to actually change our emotional state or provide any true or lasting comfort. Instead, they help us to only momentarily distract ourselves from a lower emotion or mask its expression. The result is that we keep our physical vibration low and cement our fear-based destructive patterns in our physicality. Fearful emotional patterns become fearful eating patterns.

As we move toward higher levels of consciousness, the food that appeals to us will shift and change over time. When we are in a high emotional state, we will actually crave food that will sustain a high level of vibration or consciousness in the body, such as organic produce or lean protein. Instead of engaging our conditioned pattern in relationship to food, we can now see diet as a way to establish a state of optimal well-being and increase our vitality and level of consciousness.

Conscious eating brings a practice of awareness to our daily diet that supports us in making healthy choices regarding what we eat. As we saw with the mind and emotions, awareness is the first step in transformation. To begin developing the skills necessary to transform destructive eating patterns, we must *tune in* when we are eating and drinking. By tuning in, we become aware of what is actually driving dietary choices and the impact these choices are having on our physiology.

Before eating, identify how you feel emotionally. Acknowledge the emotion that is present. Be aware of the food you desire from this emotional state. If a fearful emotional state is present, then do the work to shift the emotional pattern. If you are feeling sad, angry, or anxious, acknowledge the emotion that you are feeling, give it permission to express, engage the ninety-second rule, and then shift into a higher emotional state such as peace or joy. Once you are in that higher emotional state, then ask yourself, *What nutritional choice will best serve my body's optimal well-being and support my Conscious Transformation?*

After tuning in emotionally, now tune in physically. Ask what your level of hunger is in the body. Is there a particular craving in this moment? Make sure any such craving is not from a level of addiction but instead is a healthy communication from the body. With these questions in mind, now make the choice about what to eat that will best support the body's needs in that moment.

Halfway through the meal, tune in to the body again. What impact is this food having on the body? Does the body feel nourished and vibrant? At this point, we want to again check in with our hunger level. It is important to make sure that we quit eating when we are two-thirds full so we have the energy to properly digest our food. This is a state where you are no longer hungry but you are not yet full. If you quit eating at this point, then the body has plenty of energy to properly digest the food, and you will not be tired after you eat.

We again check in with the emotions and the body when we are finished eating, and an hour after the meal has been completed. At both of these points, be aware of the emotions that are present and the physical sensations in the body. Ask yourself how your food choice has affected your overall physical, mental, and emotional state: has it altered it at all? In what way or ways?

As you engage this process over time, look for the patterns connecting your state of being to what you are eating. For example, you may notice that after you eat bread, you become congested or fatigued. Your body may not like the wheat or may not be able to appropriately process the gluten. Become sensitive to any negative states that show up during or after a meal, and look for the connection between the state you are experiencing and the foods you were eating. Once you see such negative patterns, you can try eliminating those foods from your diet. How does that elimination affect how you feel—mentally, emotionally, and physically?

Signs that certain foods may not be serving include congestion, fatigue, pain, swelling, foggy mind, and low emotional states. Signs that foods are supporting the body include a clear mind, high emotional state, and abundant energy. By developing awareness in this manner, we can see what foods benefit our health and consciousness and what foods are detrimental to our well-being. Once we have such awareness, we can make conscious choices to eat only what is in service to our highest well-being. Through this process, we begin to create new physical patterns that support our Conscious Transformation.

With the emotions, when we came to realize how destructive our negative emotional patterns were, we could no longer sustain them. In the same way, as we begin to develop an awareness of how harmful processed and conventional foods are, it becomes increasingly difficult to eat them. As we increase our awareness of the foods we are eating and the effects they have on our bodies, we become motivated to break these destructive patterns in caring for our physical self and find the many options available that can propel us to health and vitality.

Many options now exist for establishing a healthy diet. Organic grocery stores are now prevalent, and even more mainstream grocers have aisles of organically grown produce, hormone-free and antibiotic-free meat, and health foods. People have begun to grow their own food in backyard gardens again. In the last decade, there has been a sharp rise in community-sustained agriculture, where individuals purchase a share of a farm and receive locally grown, organic food in return. Farmers' markets selling locally raised produce and meats have exploded in popularity.

It is important to note that there are a variety of different diets that serve a variety of different people. Some people eat strictly vegetarian or vegan diets, while others feel healthier when they eat meat. There is no perfect diet that fits everyone's needs. What is important is to supply your body with the proper nutrition. Conscious eating provides a system that allows us to tune in to our bodies and define what best serves our nutritional needs and our Conscious Transformation.

Perhaps we should think of the need to engage a practice of conscious eating in these terms: if you destroy your physical body, where will you live? The analysis is really that simple. The body is what keeps us here, present in this life. We cannot stay alive without a body.

Although we are not our physical bodies, they are the temples we call home during our stay in this human form. The body is the home for our consciousness, and the body influences our level of consciousness to an extent that few accurately comprehend. Therefore, we must not only attend to our bodies' needs, but we must also treat our bodies with great care and respect. In other words, attending to the health and well-being of our bodies cannot be a mere afterthought, but instead must become a high priority.

Living an active lifestyle and exercising routinely are also essential components to physical health and well-being. Our bodies were designed to move. We were never intended to have a sedentary lifestyle. In fact, one of the most destructive lifestyles we can engage in is the sedentary lifestyle currently the norm of our culture.

Although new technology has brought many benefits, its negative implications cannot be overlooked. Many members of our society now perform jobs that saddle them to a computer screen. Children *play* with video games, watch television, and text their friends for entertainment instead of running around outdoors. This sedentary lifestyle spent perched in front of electronic devices has become the norm for adults and children alike and is a major contributing factor to our declining health.

In today's world, it is very easy to let the physical body go. Taking care of ourselves physically often drops to the last item on our to-do list. Perhaps another reason that care of the physical body is so frequently subject to slipping is the full impact of our abuse of the body is not always immediate noticeable. We can go for years, particularly when we are young, failing to eat appropriately or exercise routinely, and only be aware of minor consequences resulting from such action. Ultimately, our lifestyles will catch up with us, and we will suffer as a result.

Early in my life, the lesson regarding the need to move and care for the body was driven home to me by the contrast between my grandfather and my *sifu* or teacher. When I was eighteen years old, I studied the martial-arts disciplines of Kung Fu and Qigong. At the time, both my martial-arts *sifu* and my grandfather were in their sixties, but the difference in their physical health was striking.

My sifu would awake at 6:00 a.m., teach classes, and treat clients throughout the day without pausing to rest until sometimes after midnight. My sifu could still run, kick over his head, and sit crossed-legged on the floor. Although in his sixties, he had as much energy as most of the young adults and teenagers he taught. Having been trained in the Eastern philosophy by Chinese monks in a temple in San Francisco, he had learned how to care for the body through meditation, high-nutritional practices, herbal remedies, and cultivating his internal energy through specialized forms of exercise. My sifu was a vibrant picture of health who was fully capable in his senior years of living an extraordinary life.

My grandfather, on the other hand, did not take the best care of himself nutritionally. He had followed a typical Western diet with a lot of meat and potatoes. He had smoked unfiltered Camel cigarettes every day since he was teenager. By the time he was in his mid-sixties, he was diagnosed with emphysema. One of my last memories of my grandfather is of him lying on his sofa, barely able to breathe and unable to get up to walk fifty yards to see his beloved horse. Prior to being diagnosed with emphysema, he had actually lived an active lifestyle. He was a carpenter who loved to hunt, horseback ride, and tend to the land he owned. However, due to insufficient care of his body, the body failed him at an early age.

Even at that time in my life, it was clear to me that as much as I loved my grandfather, I did not want to follow in his footsteps with regard to my own physical health. Instead, I desired to emulate my sifu, living a full life well into my later years. My sifu repeatedly taught us that keeping the body active through daily physical activity and exercise was essential for longevity and vitality. One of his core teachings was that the body was not designed to be sedentary. However, my sifu also understood that the state of the mind was intricately related to the state of the body.

So why do our thoughts and emotions also have such a profound impact on our body's health and vitality? As most of us know, our bodies are made up of trillions of cells working together in perfect harmony to sustain life. Within the cells' membranes are two classes of proteins: receptor proteins and effector proteins. Receptor proteins can be thought of as antennae that are tuned to respond to environmental signals. In each cell's membrane, there are hundreds of thousands of receptor proteins. Some receptor proteins respond to physical signals such as hormones, histamines, neurotransmitters, and other chemicals produced by our physical, mental, and emotional bodies. Other receptor proteins respond to vibrations including sound, thought, emotion, light, and radio waves. For each environmental signal that needs to be read, there is a different receptor protein.

When a receptor protein detects an environmental signal, it triggers the effector protein. At this point, the effector protein responds by actually changing the shape of the protein itself. As stem-cell biologist Bruce Lipton explains in his book, *The Biology of Belief*, the receptor and effector proteins "act as a switch, translating environmental signals into cellular behavior." As a result, Lipton and others in his field have now concluded that "the cell's operations are primarily molded by its interaction with the environment, not by its genetic code."

Once these basics of cellular function are understood, it is impossible to doubt the connection between physical, mental, and emotional health. With this understanding comes a comprehension of just how much power we have. Our bodies are constructed in a manner that empowers us to influence our lives all the way down to our basic cellular structure. No longer can we think of ourselves as prisoners of fate. Instead, this emerging science demands that we recognize the importance of our internal and external environments in molding who we are and what we experience.

This understanding requires a radical shift in how we see the world and ourselves in it. Gone are the days when we can say that the music we listen to, the television shows we watch, the movies we go to, the thoughts we secretly think, and the emotions we privately experience do not matter. Now we must own up to the fact that it all matters. It all counts. It all converges to shape our health and the health of those around us in very profound ways. With this new empowerment comes a new level of accountability.

We also must recognize that our cells, which are so deeply penetrated by internal and external forces, come into existence and die off routinely. As new cells come in, the intelligence of the old cells is passed on to the new. Therefore, if our level of consciousness is evolving, our physical bodies should be evolving to a higher state as well. Every cell currently present in our bodies will be gone within seven years and replaced by new cells. Not one cell that is here today will still be present in us after this relatively short period of time. From a biological perspective, in less than a decade, we will each be a completely different person than the one reading this book.

In understanding how changes in our bodies are effected, it is helpful to look beyond the cell. When we break down our impermanent cells, we discover that they are composed of a multitude of molecules which, when broken down, are composed of atoms. As we may remember from science class, atoms are made up of particles known as protons, neutrons, and electrons.

However, a fact that most of us did not learn in basic science is that 99.99 percent of each atom is actually empty space. We can visualize the atoms that make up our bodies as each being their own solar system containing a center nucleus composed of protons and neutrons with electrons that orbit around this nucleus in a vast, empty space. Therefore, what appears to the uneducated observer to be the solid structure of the body is mere illusion. This vision of the body's empty space can shift our perception and give us a further understanding of why we are able to shape and reshape our physicality through *mere* mental, emotional, and physical influences.

When we become aware of our bodies as some one hundred trillion cells, each containing 25,000 genes and hundreds of thousands of environmental sensing proteins that pick up all that we encounter, we begin to become aware of the vast universe of existence operating within us. We also begin to get a small sense of the potential that *is* our very existence. How we influence that creation through our internal state and our external environment establishes our level of consciousness and births our existence from our own inner universe of infinite possibility.

Our bodies are a mass of constantly changing energy comprising a multitude of energetic systems that operate on electrical impulse. Our hearts beat as a result of electrical impulses. The neurons in our brains fire, allowing us to think, as a result of electrical signals as well. Therefore, it is not surprising that the vibration that you carry in *this* body would be critical for determining how healthy you are overall. Everything that you encounter and everything that you put into your body has its own level of vibration or consciousness. Envisioning all that you encounter and consume as a vibration, and choosing whether you wish to engage something based upon its vibratory level, is a new way of thinking that can significantly impact your state of being.

When we become truly grateful for our bodies, we start to become aware of the necessity of supporting our physical structures. With gratitude, the process of shifting destructive physical patterning can become a graceful experience. In a state of gratitude, it becomes easy for us to be aware of the miracle that is the physical body.

Every moment of our existence, the body is sustaining your life so you can experience what it is to be human. Your heart never stops pumping blood throughout your body. Your lungs never stop breathing. Your organs constantly serve on your behalf. Your brain never sleeps and makes it possible for you to be self-aware. This harmonious symphony of events is constantly unfolding in the body, even when you are unaware of it taking place. No aware person making conscious choices would make it harder for the body to fulfill its awe-inspiring service that sustains one's very life.

As vast as your physical body is, your true self is a presence that transcends physicality. The body is merely a precious vessel holding within it the life force that you are so that you can have an experience on this planet. As awe-inspiring as the physical body is, the beauty of your true self is beyond comprehension.

CHAPTER 7

The Transformative Power of the Spiritual Self

Intuition is a spiritual faculty and does not explain, but simply points the way.

—FLORENCE SCOVEL SHINN

The birth of our human bodies in this life was not the beginning of our existence, nor do we cease to exist after we depart these human lives we are living. Before we were born, we existed as pure energy or consciousness. Our consciousness then took birth in the container that is our physical body. As a result of this birth, our bodies provide us the opportunity to experience life as a human being while broadcasting our frequency of individualized consciousness.

But as mystics and philosophers have long noted, we are not these bodies. They are temporary lodging at best. We are not our minds. Our minds can create stories that can trap us in states that do not serve us. We are not our emotions. Our emotions fuel the mind, creating chaos and discord while running the same destructive patterns over and over again. Even emotional expression that is of a pleasurable nature is a prison when we remain stagnant in that state and cannot evolve into higher emotional experience. In other words, we may be in a comfortable prison but it is a prison that confines us to a certain level of emotional expression and consciousness. To experience higher states of being, we must step out of our conditioned patterns, both pleasurable and painful. Although our inner matrix tries to convince us that we *are* these small, patterned, prison cells it has created, we are not our body, mind, or emotions. We are just visiting.

So who or what is it that is visiting this human form? For anyone who has been present when a loved one has died, there is an unmistakable moment when the person we loved is suddenly gone. Although the body is still there, what we identified as that person is no longer present with us. The human life ends in the moment that life force leaves the body, and without it, the body immediately begins to decay. This life force that leaves the body is the consciousness that is our spiritual self. The spiritual self is our immortal visitor.

All of the great wisdom traditions and mythologies understand and recognize the spiritual self as our true immortal being. This spiritual self provides the capacity for awareness. The mind, emotions, and physical body are merely woven into the fabric of our infinite spirit. It is our spirit that beats our hearts, fills our lungs, and animates our bodies. It is always aligned with our highest good and is in a state of absolute purity. It is the energy of pure unconditional love. It is pure, creative life force itself.

Given that the spiritual self is unlimited creative life force, one would think that our lives would be in a state of perfection. This is not the case when our unconscious mental, emotional, and physical patterning is the driving force in our lives. Over time our patterns create a prison that deprives us of access to any other way of being. This unconscious patterning creates the illusion of separation from our spiritual selves and from the people in our lives. Over time, we come to believe that these patterns within our inner matrix are our identity.

Although we are always connected to our spiritual self, our awareness and access to that connection becomes clouded by the static of our unconscious mental, emotional, and physical patterning. We can think of our spiritual self as the sun and our mental, emotional, and physical patterns as clouds. On a cloudy day, the sun is still high in the sky serving us. We are receiving the benefit of the sun even though we cannot see it.

If the clouds blocking the sun came and stayed for generations on end, after a while, people would forget what was producing the light. When others tried to remind them that the sun is responsible for the light, many would likely reject this truth. Having never seen it for themselves, they would conclude that the story of the sun was merely a myth—until one day, the wind blew away the clouds and all could see. Our mental, emotional, and physical patterns have been developed, maintained, and strengthened over generations, passed from one member of our family to the next. As a result, we can no longer see the light of the spiritual self that is present, sustaining our every breath.

For all the seeking of the spiritual aspect that goes on in this world every single day in its many and varied forms, the irony is that we are always connected to our spirit. In fact, we cannot be disconnected from this spirit and still be alive in these bodies. The ultimate truth is that *we already are everything we seek*. To experience this truth and part our own clouds, we need only to consciously transform the inner matrix and its conditioned patterns to a higher state of spiritual connection.

The inner matrix—or ego—without guidance from the higher self, functions in a fear-based state of unconscious reaction. To the inner matrix, any change is feared, even if it would relieve our suffering and transform our lives into a magical existence. The inner matrix perceives all change as a threat, even if it is positive and beneficial, because it is unknown.

It is the mental, emotional, and physical patterning we have spent so much time discussing that insists on being sustained. What is unacceptable to the inner matrix is a lack of familiarity. Familiarity reassures the inner matrix that it will survive to live another day. When we run our patterns, the outcome is predictable and the inner matrix is comfortable, even when it hurts.

With this intelligence of fear driving our unconscious reactions, the inner matrix will be aligned with aspects of fear such as anger, sadness, betrayal, jealousy, disgust, shame, and guilt. If we look at these fearful patterns as though they were living beings that wish to sustain their lives, then we can begin to understand that these patterns wish to exist and why they will fight for their survival.

For example, a new way of being, such as joy, will be a threat to anger. Anger will not go peaceably, because it knows that if joy takes over, it will cease to exist. It is impossible to be aligned with both fear and love at the same time. By directing the inner matrix in a pattern of fear, anger ensures that it will be fed, nurtured, and kept alive.

Think about someone you have known who seems to be angry all the time. Imagine if, one day, that person suddenly showed up and was no longer driven by that core pattern of anger. Instead of being cynical, judgmental, angry, pessimistic, and complaining, the person would now be joyful, loving, compassionate, and optimistic, seeing only the best in those around them. In such a situation, you would wonder what had happened to the person you knew. They simply would not be the same person they once were. As the fearful pattern of anger dissolved in their inner matrix, a part of them would have died. With that death came a rebirth. This is the power of Conscious Transformation that the inner matrix fears.

Therefore, the inner matrix keeps us from taking the internal and external actions necessary to realize our highest potential. For example, instead of stepping into a place of unconditional love and joy in our relationships, we are kept trapped in anger and frustration, convinced by the inner matrix that we need to protect or defend ourselves. Instead of leaving the job where we are stagnated and unable to utilize our skills and talents, we stay because things could always be worse. Perhaps we don't even take the first step to building a new life because we are convinced that we are not worthy or capable of doing anything different.

A strong connection to the spiritual self is essential if we wish to shift out of fear. Without a strong connection, fear is an extremely effective tool by which we can be easily manipulated. The inner matrix will seek to trap us in our prison walls and throw away the key by utilizing every fearful tool at its disposal. One of those tools is depriving us of any awareness that it is actually the inner matrix at work in our lives. In other words, the inner matrix is sneaky when it is fighting to survive.

The inner matrix may attempt to distract us from our spiritual self by manipulating us through such seemingly noble traits as devotion to family, friends, or career. What can appear at first blush to be steeped in the highest of good intentions can actually be cunning egoist distraction. It is the inner matrix aligned with fear that tells us that we can't possibly spend a weekend at a personal transformation program because we would be neglecting our family. It is the inner matrix whispering in our ear that we don't have time to work out because we have responsibilities at our job. It is the inner matrix that pushes our emotional buttons when we feel guilty sitting in meditative practice, because we are ignoring people who love us or are failing to work on our long to-do list.

The inner matrix is the ever-present voice in the back of our heads insisting that if we take time for ourselves, we are being selfish. These deceptive tactics are usually far more effective than a more obvious appeal to a baser instinct. The inner matrix manipulates us through our thoughts and emotions time and time again, triggering our unconscious patterns and turning us away from building that critical relationship with the spiritual self that enables us to consciously transform.

When we are unsure whether we are being driven by unconscious patterning from our inner matrix or by genuine guidance from our spiritual self, our emotions can serve as a litmus test. If we tune in to our emotions and find we are experiencing anger, hatred, guilt, shame, resentment, or overwhelm, then we know that the fear-based unconscious patterns of our inner matrix are driving us. If on the other hand, we tune in and find states of love, joy, peace, compassion, or harmony operating, we can be assured that the spiritual self is in charge.

Our inner matrix will also attempt to convince us that we can continue to engage our old patterns and somehow think, emote, and satiate ourselves to happiness. Nothing could be further from the truth. It is a bald-faced lie. Allowing the outside world to trigger old mental, emotional, and physical patterns leads to the same outcome and reinforces these unconscious patterns.

We may feel as though we are exercising choice, but the truth is that instead we are merely running old patterns in new situations. We take a few facts that show up in our external world, add layer upon layer of inflammatory story designed to trigger emotional reaction, and we are off to the races, time and time again. Although the situation and the faces may differ, the underlying reaction is the same, and what is created from that place will be the same as well. If our patterning continues to operate, we will not experience change.

When we live from the inner matrix, we are trapped in the prison of pattern, at the mercy of what shows up in our outside world. In this space, we are impacted by the world and often see ourselves only as a victim of our current situation. We may desire change, but because we show up time and time again in the same mental, emotional, and physical patterns, we have essentially the same experiences. Until we are willing to find another way, we are cut off from the magnificence of who we truly are. The only path out of the prison is through connection with the spiritual self. When we connect with the spiritual self, this is a place of empowerment that allows us to influence, define, and affect our inner matrix and the world around us.

Oftentimes, when spiritual authors and psychologists speak of the inner matrix or ego, it is with some disdain. This is a mistake. The inner matrix or ego is a powerful force that we must have a healthy respect for if we wish to engage in true, lasting transformation. The inner matrix is a highly intelligent force that has existed for millions of years by being both extremely powerful and cunning.

We must not look at the inner matrix as a force that needs to be destroyed. Instead, we must see it as a small child that needs training so that it won't burn down the house when it is left unsupervised for a few minutes. It is critical that we redeem the inner matrix by aligning it with love so that it will no longer undermine us, but instead will serve as our ally in personal transformation. Over time, the new mental, emotional, and physical patterns we have consciously chosen will become our default patterns and will anchor within our inner matrix. Once we reach this point, even when we do leave the inner matrix unattended, the patterns running will align with our spiritual self, thereby serving our higher good.

The good news is, because our spiritual *visitor* is capable of observing our thoughts, emotions, and physicality, we do not have to stay in our destructive unconscious patterns. From this place of observation, we can engage our process of Conscious Transformation by developing our awareness, shifting patterns that do not serve us, and practicing new states of being that transform our experience of life.

Conscious Transformation allows us to step outside of our patterns and create experiences aligned with the state of unconditional love, which is our spiritual self. Instinctively we know that thinking, feeling, and taking action in alignment with states of love, peace, and harmony will drive us to a better place within ourselves and our lives. At the same time, intuitively we also know that anger, hatred, greed, shame, and jealousy do not serve us. The spiritual self allows us to transcend and uplift our unconscious patterns. Through this connection to the spiritual, we align with the natural flow of life, effortlessly creating experiences of harmony, peace, love, and joy.

Just as being trapped in the prison of the inner matrix perpetuates stagnation, being connected to the spiritual self manifests constant evolution and expansion. Intuition is the language of our spiritual self. Intuition is an inner voice that guides us, showing us the way, even if there is no reason or rationale to support it. The conditioned patterns in our mind, emotions, and body make for perilous navigation systems that strand us in dangerous territory and will always bring us to what we have already known. However, our spiritual body is an internal GPS system that we can trust every time to help us find our way home to the dreams and visions we hold for ourselves.

If we choose to take this journey, relying on our intuition to guide us, ten years from now—or even one year from now—we will not recognize ourselves or our lives. However, the new lives that will emerge will be far greater than what we know or can even conceive of in this moment. Our fantasies of this future existence will undoubtedly fall short.

The reason we cannot accurately envision the world that will emerge when we align with a higher level of consciousness is that any visions we create for our future will be extrapolations of what we have known at our current, lower level of consciousness. The world that will emerge from this higher level of consciousness will be beyond that which we can currently conceive. We simply cannot accurately imagine what we have never experienced.

We can and should use our vision to motivate us to move forward and create beneficial changes. However, we cannot become too attached to *how* we will manifest our vision or what it will be like when we arrive at this new place. If we already knew how to create our vision, we would already be there. Therefore, it is important to be connected to our intuition so that it can guide us to this new place. Although we may not know the way, having never been there before, our intuition does know.

For example, we can imagine climbing Mount Everest, but until we actually scale the mountain and arrive at the summit, we won't truly understand the journey required to get there or what it is like to stand on its peak. We can all imagine what it would be like to visit the Great Pyramid of Giza in Egypt, but until we actually step into the King's Chamber, we cannot accurately envision the experience. We can dream of a healthy and loving relationship, but until we are actually in such a relationship, we don't know what it will be to have that fulfillment in our lives.

We cannot know until we get to a higher level of consciousness what it will be like to arrive or what it will take to get there. We must admit that we do not know what is required to take us where we wish to go. As a result, we have to step out of what we think we know and step into our spiritual self.

In order to take that step and know the spiritual self, we must surrender. In Western culture, *surrender* is a word most often used to describe defeat. An army loses a battle and is forced to surrender to save their lives. We confuse surrender with submission. We think of it as a loss of power. *Merriam-Webster's Dictionary* even defines it as "to give oneself up into the power of another, especially as a prisoner."

On a spiritual path, it is critical that we transform our understanding of what surrender is and what surrender brings. One piece of pop culture that serves as an example of spiritual surrender is the climactic moment in the first Star Wars movie. As Luke Skywalker is flying toward the evil empire's mother ship, he hears his teacher's voice say, "Use the force, Luke." In that moment, he surrenders, trusting a force greater than his limited self, and all is not lost but instead all is gained. Luke is victorious.

Like Luke, when we surrender spiritually, we are not losing anything. We have lived in the false and limited identity of the inner matrix. Now we step into our spiritual self. In this state we uncover a pure power that has gone unrecognized and unknown until the moment of surrender. In this moment, we transcend our human limitations, transform our consciousness and step into an experience of the sublime. We no longer identify with the limited confines of our inner matrix. Now we know ourselves as the infinite power of the higher self. We are in a Presence where fear cannot survive. It is the experience of life divine.

In order to obtain this new level of consciousness, we must have the willingness to let go of what is here now so that we can unlock the doors to this free and magnificent life. We cannot cling to our old ways, because answers to perceived problems on this journey of transformation cannot be found by looking to the past we have lived. Answers based on our past will only bring us more of what we have already experienced, instead of facilitating the life to which we aspire. In order to consciously transform, we must leave who we are and what does not serve behind and embrace who we are becoming and what supports that new state.

A state of surrender fueled by humble courage is what is necessary to be able to let go of that which is not serving us. This state creates a space for stepping into the unknown. It is in the unknown where we discover a higher level of consciousness that allows new experiences to arise, moving us toward states that serve us and ultimately manifesting our vision. In order to surrender, we must dare to accept the influence and direction of the spiritual in our lives. No matter the issue, the answers we seek to whatever issues we have lie just beyond the boundaries of sensation at the level of the spiritual.

As we surrender our inner matrix, the answers will come as our consciousness evolves. We must allow our spiritual self to guide us on this path of transformation. We also must trust and have faith that our intuition and spirit will bring us to our destination in a way that serves our highest good and manifests our unrealized potential. Given that our spiritual self is always aligned with our highest good, when we follow its guidance, taking action from our intuition, we can be assured that we are on the right path.

When we surrender to our Conscious Transformation with devotion and sincerity, a strong connection to the spiritual will bring the people and circumstances to us that we need to become who and what we were meant to be on this planet. No matter what we are trying to do, the spiritual will guide us—whether it is building a meaningful relationship or becoming a better lawyer.

Once we start to open ourselves to the spiritual, we must allow it to guide us like a huge tidal wave in the ocean. We cannot resist, or the wave will crush us. Ride it and it will take us to new heights in every aspect of our lives. The power that lives in this space of the spirit is limitless. Through meditation, we access our spiritual self, tune in to it, and begin harnessing that inner power to focus a tidal wave of energy toward manifesting our vision.

Through meditation, we can learn to transcend the mind and increase our connection with spirit. In this practice, we focus on our center. Our center is a spot two inches below the belly button and an inch back toward the spine. Close your eyes and begin breathing through your nose with your mouth closed and your tongue touching the palate of your mouth. Breathe into your center and envision your breath as golden light. Giving color to your breath helps to give your brain something to focus on and offers a way to visualize the life force that dwells within you.

Next, imagine a column or tube of light descending down into the top of your head and extending all the way down into your center. You will see an image of yourself in the center of that tube, ascending higher and higher until you go all the way out the top of your head and connect with a huge source of energy, light, and spirit. Imagine breathing that energy down the tube all the way into your center. Breathe into that light and see the light expand through your body. In that space of connection, continue to breathe for twenty minutes. When thoughts, emotions, and sensations come up, just acknowledge them and gently return your focus back to your visualization.

Through this meditative practice, you will learn how to silence the mental and emotional chatter and gain access to your spiritual self. Because the spiritual self is pure consciousness, this visitor within operates on a level of divine or super intelligence. Over time, you will build a strong relationship with your spiritual self. As you become able to enter this space at will, you will be able to access a powerful tool to guide you in consciously creating your life.

When you come to a fork in your road and it is necessary to make a critical decision about which way to turn, you can tap into the high intelligence of your spiritual self and ask for guidance. Now you have choice. In this space, you can listen and then take conscious action rooted in the information you receive, instead of regressing into old patterns. Because you are connecting with an infinite source of power and intelligence that exists in a state of absolute purity, there is no boundary between who you can become and no ceiling on what you can create. You are now breaking free from your prison. In this space, anything is possible.

CHAPTER 8

The Mirror

Love in its essence is spiritual fire.

—LUCIUS ANNAEUS SENECA,
ROMAN PHILOSOPHER

All that is possible in our external world is controlled by our internal state of being. As we have discussed, most of us believe that we are at the mercy of what shows up in our external environment. We mistakenly believe that our families, friends, jobs, and the other happenings in our world create our lives. The majority of us cannot see the connection between our unconscious patterning and what shows up in our lives because we lack an awareness of our own patterns, let alone the impact they are having on how we experience the world.

Because these unconscious patterns are in control and we lack awareness of them, most of us are completely unable to see ourselves. Events occur in our lives, and they trigger our unconscious emotional patterning. Unbeknownst to us, the emotional pattern fuels the mind to create a story that supports or justifies what is usually an undesirable lower emotion. We then react. By saying or doing something in alignment with the pattern that is operating at that time, we create our experience.

As we discussed earlier, each emotional state has its own intelligence and, therefore, its own creative power. If we act from a state of anger, the action we take will most likely be regrettable, and what we create will be as well. Remember, when we are angry, or in alignment with any fear-based emotional pattern, we are stupid—because from these states we cannot possibly create what we desire in this world. As we explained previously, when we are under the influence of the reptilian brain, we simply do not have access to the higher states of being that are directed by the prefrontal cortex. From the reptilian brain state, we can create more anger, guilt, shame, or resentment, but we cannot create love, peace, compassion, joy, or harmony. Higher states of consciousness simply cannot be created from lower emotions.

As a result, we are limited in what we can manifest in our world. We may desire a loving, compassionate, and peaceful relationship, but if our unconscious patterns are operating, we are not going to get it. As a result, we become like the ball in a pinball machine, bouncing off everything that shows up, unable to direct or control our own destiny but certain that others are to blame for the state of our lives.

The best place to begin to see ourselves is through our relationships. Believe it or not, relationships are the most effective tool we have to pierce the veil of unconsciousness and provide us with an up-close and personal look at what actually dwells within us. When we come to understand that our relationships are truly just mirrors of our internal states of being, they become a powerful tool for our own Conscious Transformation.

As we know, all the experiences we have in our various relationships are unfolding and happening inside of us. Our external environments simply do not create them. The people in our lives are just triggering an inner experience that existed inside of us long before those people entered our lives. When we recognize that what shows up in our relationships is a reflection of what is happening inside us, we accelerate the speed at which we can develop our awareness of our unconscious patterning. As we expand our awareness, we can use our relationships as tools to consciously transform ourselves. Through this process, we can move our relationships into a higher and even magical state.

We think we are having different relationships with different people, but in truth, because our unconscious internal patterning drives us, these relationships are only a projection of our own internal states of being. We are first and foremost in relationship with ourselves, and all our external relationships are a projection of this most important relationship. This is why the relationships in our lives act as mirrors. As Joseph Campbell noted in *Reflections on the Art of Living*, "The universe is a great spread-out net with, at every joint, a gem and each gem not only reflecting all the others but itself reflected in all."

As we react to those we are in relationship with, we are merely seeing our internal patterns reflected back to us through that person. Our external world is merely mirroring what lives inside of us. If we see anger in the person we are in relationship with, it is because that pattern dwells within us. It may not be expressed in the same way our partner is expressing it, or it may lie deep within our unconscious patterns, but somewhere within our inner matrix, that ghost haunts our existence. Our entire external world is a mirror, but our close relationships reflect the most powerful magnification of our internal selves.

Although we often blame others we are in relationship with for failing to meet our needs, we haven't really been in relationship with the other person. Instead, we have just been in relationship with the experience of our own old patterns. Until we step out of our patterns, the people we are in relationship with and the actions they take are fairly irrelevant to our experience. One way or another, our inner matrix will find a justification for running our unconscious patterns, allowing us to stay locked safely in our prison cells.

When we begin to accept our relationships as the mirrors they truly are, suddenly all blame is gone. Because relationships are here as a tool to show us what lives inside us so that we can attend to those patterns, how can we be angry or disappointed at the person we are in relationship with? After all, the *problems* that we see in others are a reflection and illumination of our own areas of internal existence that need to be shifted and transformed in order that we might experience something different. With acceptance of this truth comes a new level of accountability but also a new level of empowerment.

In order to truly connect with another human being in a manner that does not bring pain into our lives and does not strengthen patterns that do not serve us, we must learn to define our internal state and influence the relationship consciously. Clearly, we cannot connect to another person through our higher states of being such as love, joy, compassion, and peace unless we take the time and effort to strengthen these patterns within our inner matrix.

Ultimately, there are three aspects to every relationship: our end, the other person's end, and the relationship itself. It is not our job to take responsibility for the other person's end of the relationship. What they put into the relationship is their responsibility. We can only take responsibility and accountability for what we feed the relationship.

As human beings, our single greatest desire is the desire to connect. This desire is fueled by the desire to be loved. Most of us engage in relationships because we wish to be loved by another. However, for most of us, love at the level of relationship is conditional love, fueled by emotions and tied to needs, wants, and desires. When the people we are in relationship with meet our needs, wants, and desires, we accept that we love them and that they love us. All is good. As soon as a need, want, or desire goes unmet, however, we feel angry, disappointed, frustrated, and betrayed. We tell ourselves that if the person loved us, meeting our needs would have been a top priority. We no longer feel the experience of loving the other person or of being loved. In most relationships, that feeling of love simply comes and goes.

Conditional love is a type of bartered relationship. We agree to love someone, but only with the expectation that the other person provides us with certain things that we need, want, or desire. As a matter of fact, most of us enter relationships to begin with because we want to find something we do not have. We want to feel loved. We want a companion so that we will no longer feel lonely. We desire to have someone entertain us, so that we will no longer be sad. Unfortunately, because a relationship is a mirror of our own state of being, it can never give us what we do not already possess.

Many people believe love to be connection even if the connection is coming from a state of lower vibration such as anger, jealousy, or resentment. Even though we may be resonating with another person and there is a *sense* of connection, we should not confuse this with love.

If we understand how we attract relationships into our lives, the absurdity of our expectation that someone can give us what we lack becomes even clearer. Relationships are based upon the law of resonance.

The term *resonance* is sometimes used in astrophysics to describe a *synchronous gravitational relationship.* Although the astrophysicists are talking about planets instead of people, the saying holds true: "as above, so below." Because we resonate with those who have the same patterns as we do in their inner matrix, we are attracted to those people who are vibrating on our same level.

Consciousness attracts *like consciousness.* It is a law of this universal existence. If we hold a strong emotional pattern of anger, the people we will be attracted to and feel the greatest connection to and resonance with will be those who are angry. It is only possible to experience a deep connection to those who are resonating in the same frequency as we are. If we vibrate in a state of joy, we will feel attracted to and resonate with others who are joyful. When we are around people who are angry, we will simply not be attracted or connected to them. Instead, we will want to keep our distance from them.

We can use the analogy of radio stations to understand resonance. With radio stations, the radio waves are always present. Like radio transmitters, people put out vibrations on a specific wavelength or frequency. If we are driving our car and we tune in to a certain frequency on the radio, then we can hear what is on that radio station. If we tune into a station that plays heavy metal but we want to hear classical music, we may wait an eternity to hear Beethoven. The better approach is to change the channel to a station that plays classical music. The person who enjoys listening only to heavy metal music is going to have a very difficult time convincing the classical music enthusiast to tune in to his heavy metal station. It is like mixing oil and water.

When we shift out of our destructive patterns like anger and jealously and into healthier ways of being such as joy and peace, we will see our outside world transform, because the law of resonance will dictate change. Those people and circumstances that were connected to us through the resonance of anger or jealously will now have to change their resonance and tune in to our new frequency of joy and peace in order to continue to connect with us. If they do not tune in to our new frequency, there will no longer be an attraction to that person or a resonance with them.

Through Conscious Transformation, we can use our relationships to see what stations we are tuning into. If we are angry with those we are in relationship with, the relationship is showing us our own pattern of anger. As we have said, the relationship is merely mirroring our internal state. When we become aware of what is being mirrored to us, we acknowledge where we are and shift and change our own internal state of being through our practices of Conscious Transformation. We do not try to change the other person. Trying to change the other person is like trying to stop a crime by shooting the victim instead of the perpetrator. The criminal will merely go on to commit another crime. Nothing has been solved.

We have all tried changing other people. How many countless hours have we spent analyzing what was wrong with those we were in relationship with and how we could fix them? Although this strategy fails time and time again, most of us persist in it anyway, merely intensifying the issues. The more we focus on the other person's *problem*—which is really our own patterning—the more we intensify that patterning within ourselves and the stronger it appears in our relationship.

When we project our unconscious patterning onto others, we experience the emotion inside of us. Because we are disconnected from the emotion, we are not aware that the emotion is actually inside of us. Instead, we believe that the individuals around us are expressing the emotion and that it is their issue or pattern instead of our own. In other words, we project our own emotional state onto the circumstances and individuals within our lives, unaware that the emotion actually dwells inside of us.

Therefore, if we are angry, we will project the emotion of anger onto our partner, and we will be convinced either that *she* is the angry one or that we are justified in being angry at her. If we are sad and depressed, those we are in relationship with will appear sad and depressed to us as well—or we will convince ourselves of the reasons we are entitled to be sad and depressed. In the end, we will have done nothing more than reinforce the destructive mental and emotional patterns in our inner matrix that were damaging the relationship in the first place.

Projection does nothing to alleviate the underlying emotion we have disconnected from. Instead, it actually reinforces the emotional pattern within us. As we project the emotion onto someone else, we are feeding the emotion inside of us. As we discussed before, emotion feeds and thrives on the same emotion. When we project an emotion onto someone else, it is *our* emotional state that we are in relationship with. We are not in relationship with the other person. Therefore, we are feeding and expanding the emotion that we cannot face and making it the reality of our relationships and our lives in general. Even if we decided to leave the relationship, we would attract the same dynamic to us in our next relationship because we would still internally resonate with the same patterns.

To better understand how disconnection and projection function, it may be helpful to think of the disconnected emotion as a movie and the relationship as the image that appears on the screen. If we don't like the ending of the movie and attempt to change its outcome by altering the screen, we will not be successful. Instead, the movie will continue to play and the story will be the same.

We can only change the image on the screen by altering the film itself, but if we don't have access to the film in the movie projector, we are powerless to stop the movie or change it in any way. No matter how much we protest, the movie continues to run. Because emotion drives the mind, the projection of a problem in our life is only a mirage. If we want to change the projection, we have to change its source, which is the emotion that dwells within us.

The solution is to keep the focus on our own internal state. The fact of the matter is that there is no need for us to work on or try to change other people. Repeat: there is no need for us to work on or try to change other people. We transform our relationships by shifting and changing *ourselves*. This is how we heal and evolve our relationships. When we transform our level of consciousness by shifting and changing out of our own destructive patterning, our relationships automatically transform.

When we come to resonate in a new place, our relationships are not the only thing to transform. Instead our entire lives change because we carry our new resonance into every situation we encounter. The secret to healthy relationships and transforming our lives lies in the wisdom of Gandhi who said, "We but mirror the world. All the tendencies present in the outer world are to be found in the world of our body. If we could change ourselves, the tendencies in the world would also change. As a man changes his own nature, so does the attitude of the world change towards him. This is the divine mystery supreme. A wonderful thing it is and the source of our happiness. We need not wait to see what others do."

Remember our stories about Kirk and Caroline? What we didn't disclose earlier is that Kirk and Caroline are a couple. The two have been married for fourteen years and have two daughters, but their relationship was on the brink of divorce when they met me. As you may recall, Kirk's mother had core patterns of shame, anger, resentment, abandonment, and guilt, which she imprinted on Kirk. As a result, throughout Kirk's life, he resonated with these core patterns. Of course, Kirk was attracted to Caroline because she carried these same core patterns.

Although we spoke in an earlier chapter of how Caroline's mind operated, we did not discuss her underlying emotional patterns. Caroline's mother, Mary, was a nun who dropped out of the convent and got pregnant with Caroline while dating the local college basketball star. Mary was from a strict, Irish Catholic background. Mary's parents were irate and resentful when she left the convent and furious with her for getting pregnant. Shame and guilt were the primary emotions in Mary's home environment, and when she became pregnant with Caroline, they were the two most frequently expressed. Mary gave Caroline up for adoption two weeks after she was born. However, the emotional body begins to form when we are in our birth mother's womb, and as a result,

Caroline was imprinted with shame, anger, resentment, abandonment, and guilt.

Now we can see why this couple resonated with each other. When Caroline and Kirk first met, as it is for most of us in the beginning of our relationships, everything was perfect. Both Caroline and Kirk put their best foot forward, and they fell madly in love. The pair dreamed of the blissful existence they would create together. Both had previously failed long-term relationships, but this one would be different. This time, they would live happily ever after. Little did they know that the same patterns that had destroyed their previous relationships were still active inside of them. The emotional ghosts that neither Kirk nor Caroline could see in themselves would return with a vengeance.

When Kirk and Caroline had their first daughter, Kirk felt abandoned and withdrew from Caroline. In turn, Caroline felt abandoned by Kirk. This unconscious pattern of abandonment caused them both to construct stories about how each had been wronged by the other. Their unconscious patterns of anger justified behavior toward one another that fed their mutual patterns of anger, guilt, shame, and resentment. As they ran these destructive internal patterns and played them out with each other over and over again, the patterns increased in strength. Over a period of a few short years, the happily-ever-after vision was long gone.

Although they saw two different marriage counselors, these patterns went unattended and unchanged in the two of them. As a result, these were the primary patterns that drove their relationship to the brink of divorce. Of course, Caroline could see that Kirk was angry, resentful, and full of shame and guilt. Kirk could see the same thing in Caroline. In the beginning, however, neither one could see the anger, resentment, shame, or guilt in themselves. They were unaware that their relationship was the perfect mirror of their internal selves.

Caroline heard of my work through an employee of hers and came to one of my programs. After learning about many of the techniques presented in this book, Caroline decided to engage a practice of Conscious Transformation. She was committed to changing herself and creating a better existence for her family. In the beginning, she wanted a divorce, but I convinced her to stay. I explained to Caroline that she was free to leave Kirk but that if she left without first addressing her own patterns, she would repeat them in her next relationship. Despite the fact that Kirk was not willing to do the work, Caroline persisted on her own.

As Caroline stepped further into her Conscious Transformation practices, she began to become aware of the conditioned patterns that did not serve her and started to resonate on a different level. She began to step out of anger and resentment and no longer resonated with these patterns. She shifted and changed her deeply held patterns of shame and guilt and stopped connecting on these levels. She began to experience states of peace, love, and joy for the first time in her life.

Instead of being happy that Caroline was becoming healthier, Kirk was resistant. He told Caroline that she wasn't herself any more. He did not like the changes that she was making. He did not feel connected with her anymore and experienced a feeling of greater and greater distance from his wife, because there was no longer a resonance between them. His anger intensified as it struggled to survive and attempted to maintain the status quo with her.

Caroline was no longer fighting with Kirk or blaming him for the state of their marriage. She was moving into a state of compassion and joy that Kirk could not resonate with. These new states in Caroline could not feed his core pattern of anger. Finally, in desperation, Kirk threatened to leave her if she continued with the work. Caroline persisted with her practices anyway, understanding that the only change that was possible was from within herself.

Finally, Kirk decided to come to one of my talks, to let me know how angry he was with me and how ridiculous he thought my work was. But instead of engaging me from this state of anger and blame, something shifted inside of him. When Kirk walked out of my program, he turned to Caroline and said, "You know, this guy makes a lot of sense." Although he thought that he was going to my talk to tell me off, his inner matrix had already been shifting to a higher state.

Because Kirk's mirror neurons had been connecting with Caroline's, a new state had already begun to take hold in him. Although he could only justify coming to the program to take a stand, his neurology had a completely different agenda. As discussed above, the brain's mirror neurons cannot tell the difference between our having an experience and watching another person have that experience. The reaction in the brain is the same. Kirk was changed as a result of the imprints he received simply by being in relationship with Caroline. The truth is that it was only a matter of time until he began to resonate on higher levels in his own inner experience. Once he focused on himself and began to do the practices included in this book, he too quickly shifted out of his destructive patterns and began to resonate at new levels.

Through her practices, Caroline had created a space and was able to hold that consciousness no matter what showed up in her environment. As a result, she began to shake up her environment instead of having her environment shaking her up. If Kirk was angry or her kids were throwing a fit, Caroline was able to stay in a state of compassion. The state she created allowed him to begin to step out of fear and step into his true nature of love. Her new vibratory level created a space to allow her relationships to grow, evolve, and transcend.

From the very beginning, both Caroline and Kirk had desired a sense of connection and wanted desperately to be loved. The problem was that neither one had been taught how to access love and build a healthy relationship. They were both trying to get the love they lacked in their internal states by looking to an outside relationship. This strategy was flawed from the start. Because of the law of resonance, both Caroline and Kirk could only be in a relationship with someone who was unable to express love in a healthy way and held the patterns of anger, guilt, shame, abandonment, and resentment.

Because both partners in the couple engaged the Conscious Transformation practices in this book, they could step into states of love, compassion, and joy together. As they tuned in to the frequency of love, compassion, and joy within themselves, they strengthened these patterns in each other. Now Caroline and Kirk could connect with each other on an entirely new level.

When Caroline began her work, she deeply desired to be loved unconditionally by her husband. Kirk did not have the capacity to love unconditionally, because it was not something that he had ever received. Once she stopped desiring his love and instead focused on loving Kirk freely and without condition, Caroline found that unconditional love she had searched for within herself. As a result, she received what she had longed for her entire life. As Kirk experienced being loved freely and without condition by his wife, he became able to offer that same unconditional love to her.

Other aspects of basic neurology explain why Conscious Transformation has such a profound potential to positively impact our relationships. The brain's limbic system, which plays a critical role with regard to emotion, is what is referred to as an *open system*. We have both open and closed systems in our brains. We can think of a closed system as being akin to a racetrack. There is not a beginning or an end. The entire process is self-contained. An open system, on the other hand, does not fuse and is not self-contained. Instead, it is open to and actually links with others. This is how and why we connect through relationship. Because the limbic system is an open system, it not only allows us to connect with the world around us on an emotional level, but it also allows us to impact those we are in relationship with. This is yet another reason why Caroline's work had such a profound impact on Kirk.

The brain's limbic system actually senses our environment before the brain can see what is present. The *ventral vagus nerve* runs between the brainstem and the heart. It perceives the sound of people's voices and their facial expressions. When the ventral vagus perceives that someone is in a state of peace by noticing such expressions as a softening of facial muscles or relaxation in another person's tone of voice, it senses that it is safe to connect.

Studies have shown that when the ventral vagus is activated, we have a greater capacity to listen and tune in to those around us. Caroline's new states of peace and compassion caused Kirk's ventral vagus nerve to signal that all was safe. As a result, Caroline's new state created a space for Kirk to step out of old fight-or-flight patterns and into new states of being. When Kirk no longer felt threatened, he could align with higher emotional states.

Today, Caroline and Kirk have a happy and fulfilling marriage. They are able to provide the loving, peaceful, and supportive environment they had always wanted for their daughters. Both of their careers are thriving, and they are very passionate about what they do. All aspects of their lives have transformed, and they are living their visions.

Although what happened for this couple is what happens in most situations, there are those rare individuals who are so entrenched in their fear-based patterns that they cannot change. Some of these individuals are not ready in the moment, but because the work of Conscious Transformation plants seeds of change, these individuals will seek out transformation in the future. A few will never be ready for the work in this lifetime.

Know that if we are connected to our spiritual self, we are aligned with our highest good. Whatever happens in that space of alignment will serve us. Therefore, if a relationship falls out of our lives, we allow it to go, holding our new state of unconditional love. We know that in time, if we choose to step into another relationship, the law of resonance will cause us to attract someone who holds our new, higher states of consciousness. As a result, in the new relationship, we will be able to create something quite different and quite magnificent.

So what is this love that Kirk and Caroline craved and that we all seek? When we first fall in love or have a baby, sometimes we experience a glimpse of unconditional love in a moment of purity. We love for the sake of loving. There is no judgment, criticism, or expectation. We love that person *just because*. For a moment, we see that person's true beauty, and in that experience, our spiritual self is revealed. In this moment, we believe that the unconditional love we experience came from outside ourselves and was tied to this other person.

Unbeknownst to most of us, the love that every human being truly craves is the love that comes from that connection to our own spiritual self. The love that we desire is the pure unconditional love only found in these higher levels of consciousness. This love exists inside of ourselves, but until we realize it, we cannot experience it at will or offer it to another. Only this unconditional love satisfies our deepest of human desires.

Because we have been creating our relationships from our unconscious mental, emotional, and physical patterns, these patterns have clouded our connection to the spiritual self. As a result, we no longer experience the unconditional love that is the essence of our spiritual self. We experience a feeling of being cut off. Because we cannot see what is actually causing this yearning, we mistakenly look to the outside world to fill the hole we are experiencing. Lacking the experience of pure love, as the old song goes, we go *looking for love in all the wrong places.*

We attempt to fill our need for love by connecting to other human beings instead of first connecting to our spiritual self. Of course, due to the law of resonance, we will attract someone who cannot give us what we lack, because they too will lack the quality we desire. This misplaced yearning for connection is so strong that even when we lack the skills to connect on a healthy, fulfilling, and joyful level, we connect anyway. We connect even if that connection causes us great pain and suffering— and when we are in a place of unconscious patterning, that is almost a guarantee. We encourage and continue to engage in painful relationships just to have a sense of resonance with someone or something. We have confused love with the connection that we experience with other people through our unconscious patterns.

When we lack access to our spiritual self and connect to another person from that place of longing, we can never find what we are looking for. Because we were that formless consciousness in a state of pure unconditional love before we came into this human existence, we have an innate memory of the love we are. As a result, we are always disappointed when the person we are in relationship with is unable to love us in the way we desire to be loved. We feel betrayed when the connection we experience is not the love that we remember in the core of our being. Ultimately, we blame the other person, although it is not the other person's fault. The problem is that we lack access to our spiritual self and therefore are not experiencing the unconditional love that is within us.

Because we were unconditional love before we stepped into our human existence, and because it still dwells within us today in our spiritual self, we all seek to experience this state of unconditional love again. When we engage a practice of Conscious Transformation and begin to step into these higher levels of love, peace, and joy, even if others around us are not aware of the effect it is having on them, there is still an intuitive recognition of this consciousness. At first, the inner matrix attempts to stay in a state of fear and resists these higher states of consciousness to maintain the status quo. In most cases, intuition will ultimately begin to drive our loved ones toward an experience of this higher resonance for themselves. As a result, we transform our relationships by consciously transforming our own inner matrix.

Kirk didn't know his real reason for wanting to attend my talk, but his intuition brought him where he needed to be in order to evolve. Kirk knew that he wanted a loving relationship with his wife, but he didn't know how to get there. He had no idea that the love he sought was within him, and that once he connected to his spiritual self, he would be able to experience unconditional love with her. On the other hand, his intuition knew exactly what he needed. As we begin to consciously engage our intuition and allow it to guide us, we can greatly accelerate our transformation, bringing into manifestation the dreams, goals, and visions we have for ourselves.

In order to evolve our relationships, what is necessary is a commitment to embody a state of compassion, joy, and peace regardless of what presents itself in our environments. When a trigger for one of our emotional patterns appears in our relationships, it is important to be mindful and present with what is going on in that moment. When it does, take a moment and do the work of Conscious Transformation before engaging the partner, friend, coworker or anyone else who triggers the unwanted pattern. Touch your tongue to the roof of your mouth and focus on your center. Then take one to three deep breaths into your center, and set the intention to connect with the spiritual self and the unconditional love that you carry. In that moment, focus on activating compassion and peace. Then do your best to respond to the triggering situation while maintaining this higher state. This practice calms the ventral vagus nerve and sends signals to your brain that you are safe, further fostering a peaceful state within and supporting those around you in the process to shift out of their unconscious patterning as well.

When we expand our awareness and fortify our connection to the spiritual, we build a relationship with our true nature of unconditional love. It is this relationship with the spiritual self that transforms our entire state of being. Through the work of accessing the spiritual self, the inner matrix will begin to shift and change. As these changes occur, we will transform all the relationships in our lives. It is the relationship with our *visitor*—that is, our spiritual self—that is the most important of all relationships and the one with the greatest hand in all we experience during this lifetime.

It is from this space of connection to the spiritual that we experience the ultimate truth with the most powerful transformative potential for ourselves and, therefore, our relationships. That truth is that we are all connected to everything in this web of life. As Martin Luther King, Jr. said, "It really boils down to this: that all life is interrelated. We are all caught in an inescapable network of mutuality, tied into a single garment of destiny. Whatever affects one directly, affects all indirectly."

This unconditional love or spirit connects all and is innate within all things. The life force that exists in one human being is the same life force that exists in all of humanity. This same life force also exists in the trees of the forests, the depths of our oceans, and the animals in the wild. It is the power that sustains the perfect conditions on Mother Earth to support life. It aligns the planets and the stars in perfect harmony.

All life forms are different manifestations of the same intelligence that brought pure formless energy into form. It is what physicists are searching for when they speak of a *God particle* that gives mass to creation out of a void of pure empty space. It is what mystics seek a deeper connection to, what the religious pray for, and what every one of us, on some level, yearns to experience and remember.

When we come to realize that we are truly at one with all who we are in relationship with, then the good and bad we see in others becomes merely a reflection of ourselves. From this place, there is no blame. There is only one, so there cannot be anyone outside ourselves to blame. From this space it becomes impossible to verbally, emotionally, or physically harm another. To do so would harm ourselves, because there is no other to harm. In this space, compassion, peace, and love become the natural flow. Our relationships become as they were always intended to be: a harmonious dance in the creation of life.

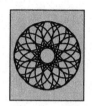

CHAPTER 9

The Individual's Role in Humanity's Evolution

Our ancient experience confirms at every point that everything is linked together, everything is inseparable.

—HIS HOLINESS THE DALAI LAMA

As we engage the process of Conscious Transformation and move into higher states, we actually become someone else. As we shift out of states of unconscious patterning and into conscious awareness, we create new states of being, and we become a new person in the process. As we connect to Presence, we experience the divine love that we truly are, and we are changed at our core. The person we are becoming is not the person we are.

As we come to new states of love, joy, peace, and compassion, we see the world through the lens of the new person we have become. As a result, our world begins to look very different, although our world has stayed exactly the same. It is only our perception of the world that has changed. Because perception creates our reality, our experience in the world radically changes when our perception changes.

The science of neuroplasticity and epigenetics shows us just how susceptible we are to change. The old phrase "you can't teach an old dog new tricks" has been disproven by this new science of empowerment. Neuroplasticity and epigenetics teaches us that we can evolve ourselves at any age and that our bodies were created to support such an evolution. We can change the wiring in our brains through simple, daily meditative practices. We can change our genetic expression through meditation, diet, and exercise. Because our cells sense everything in our environment, when we make changes in our lifestyles, we change all the way down to the cellular structure.

As we begin to embody new states of being, we become a powerful force on our environment and have a powerful impact on those closest to us. As we saw with the example of Kirk and Caroline, our neurology is created to specifically foster connection with one another. Through the mirror neurons and our open limbic system, we have the potential to deeply affect those we are in relationship with, on a physiological level. The neurology of the people in our lives is changed in a tangible way when we begin to consciously transform.

Philosophers and scientists alike have recognized the undeniable phenomenon that we are all connected in this human existence. As poet John Donne said, "No man is an island, entire of itself. Every man is a piece of the continent. Entire of the main." As Einstein similarly noted, man's experience of separateness is "a kind of optical delusion of his consciousness." Although intellectually we may understand what Donne and Einstein were referencing, we cannot experience this truth without stepping into our spiritual selves. Because so many of us lack a strong connection to the spiritual, more often than not, we do not give credence to the full impact that we have on other people and on the world at large.

Because we are all connected in this web of life, what alters one in the field of consciousness impacts the whole. As a result, if one person begins to evolve his or her level of consciousness, it supports the whole of humanity to change. Whether we can acknowledge it or not, our internal work has a global perspective. If we wish to have a positive influence on this world, the place we begin is by going inside ourselves.

We can think of what happens when a drop of water falls in the center of a still pond. The ripples expand from that little drop, circle after circle, expanding farther and farther outward. Intellectually, it is hard to imagine that a small drop of water could have such a reverberation, but most of us have witnessed this phenomenon firsthand.

When we place a thought, emotion, or action into our collective field of consciousness, it ripples like the drop of water until it reaches the shores. All that is in the field is impacted as the wave moves through our collective consciousness. The drops that we place into the field in the form of thought, emotion, and action alter the field itself, and therefore all of our human family.

As we desire to be connected to higher and higher states of being and move into these states, we remind others of the brilliance that lives within them. As we go out into the world, we begin to sow the seeds of our new state of being. When we go to the grocery store and interact with the shoppers and the clerks, instead of planting seeds of anger and resentment, we plant seeds of love and compassion. When we interact with our coworkers, we foster states of peace and harmony. When we play with our children in a state of joy, freedom, and unconditional love, we imprint them with these higher states.

When we walk as a presence of love and others enter our field of consciousness, through resonance, the quality of love is activated in those that we encounter. We have all had the experience of being in a bad mood, encountering a genuinely joyful person, and having their smile trigger that warm feeling inside of us. We all understand how one act of compassion can brighten our entire day. Just a kind word from a stranger can oftentimes part the clouds and allow the sun's warmth to flow into our lives. This is the power of the spiritual self that we carry to influence others.

As we evolve, we begin to attract new and different kinds of people and experiences to us. Through the law of attraction, our new states of being pull very different kinds of people and situations into our lives. Situations where we used to resonate no longer fit us. The environments we now attract will serve to manifest our new visions. We no longer resonate with people who vibrate at lower frequencies. The people we now attract into our lives vibrate with expressions of love, peace, compassion, and joy. Those who remain connected to us evolve, grow, and change as well.

As we move into higher and higher states of being, we truly begin manifesting and creating our world from the inside out. We begin to impact the world at large through our connection to the spiritual and its essence of divine love. As a result, we remind others of the unconditional love that is their spiritual essence as well. This remembrance supports others to step into their own transformations. We ultimately have the potential to influence millions, through merely doing our own work of Conscious Transformation.

Our history has known great leaders who have moved into high states of human capacity, sometimes known as enlightenment or self-realization. But the time for one exceptional person moving into this state has come to an end. The future of our humanity requires that entire communities now move into these exceptionally high states of being. The time has come for families and communities to support each other in Conscious Transformation so that, ultimately, the entire human race can move into this expanded state. As the renowned anthropologist Margaret Mead said, "Never underestimate the power of a few committed people to change the world. Indeed, it is the only thing that ever has." It is also the only thing that ever will.

Today, our nature is not the same as our ancestors' nature. We have evolved beyond where we were a thousand or even a hundred years ago. Science is now revealing what the great mystics have always known: there is no reason to wait for evolution. We can evolve now, in this lifetime. We have an unparalleled opportunity to step into and take part in the evolution of the human family by just stepping into these greater capacities within ourselves. By practicing Conscious Transformation, we show others the way to the states they intuitively long to experience in this human body. Over time, our individual change becomes humanity's change.

The West teaches, "The only constant is change." The East speaks in terms of impermanence and acceptance that everything in life is impermanent. People, places, situations, and even the very cells that construct our bodies come and go routinely. The foundation for life is one of constant change. It is the basic operating system for human existence. The great masters, philosophers, and prophets were right when they noted that impermanence is the permanent state of life.

Far from being a negative reality, the truth is that change is to be embraced. As science shows us, change is the very building block upon which existence in the physical body is built. In every moment, everything in the universe is either expanding or contracting. When we accept the fact that life is impermanent and we step into our power to create new and dynamic lives in each moment, we experience great expansion. On the other hand, when we fear change and resist the unknown, we contract. By trying to hold on to life as we know it, we work against life's natural flow, unwittingly embracing death.

When we shift our perspective on change, we can suddenly see that the fact that nothing is permanent brings with it infinite potential and possibility. Once we begin to work with the system of constant change instead of rejecting it, we discover that we are all empowered with the ability to shift any aspect of our lives that fails to align with our vision. Embracing change is a critical step to becoming the creator of our own existence.

As we assume responsibility for creating our lives, it is of vital importance that we become ever more vigilant about our practices of Conscious Transformation. Socrates, the father of Western philosophy, said, "The unexamined life is not worth living." This bold pronouncement is of the crucial importance to leading a conscious existence that is constantly focused inward. We must embrace this critical wisdom teaching if we wish to continue to evolve on our path of Conscious Transformation.

The foundation for living a conscious life is knowing our mental, emotional, physical, and spiritual selves. Cultivating a deep knowledge and appreciation of all aspects of the inner matrix is what facilitates our existence in this world at the highest levels of consciousness possible. Many wish to focus on the spiritual first, without taking that critical time to get to know the other three aspects. But it is this deep, abiding knowledge of the mental, emotional, and physical bodies that serves as the foundation for expansion of the spiritual self.

Without a profound understanding of how the mental, emotional, and physical operate, we slumber through life, unaware of who we actually are and unable to see how we are truly impacting the world. Absent this understanding, we can never know whether our conditioned patterns or the higher aspects of our spiritual self are running the show. We can only be certain that we are feeding our highest levels of consciousness when we bring light to those conditioned patterns that can thrive only in the shadows of unconsciousness.

Therefore, as we engage our daily lives, we must tune in to our thoughts, emotions, and sensations to ensure that we are aware of what patterns we are running. If our conditioned mental, emotional, or physical patterning is not aligned with our highest vision, then we must take time to do our practices in the moment, shifting the patterns to align with our spiritual self before we take any action. We must consistently tune in to the aspects of our inner matrix to ensure that we are on the path of engaging only what supports our optimal health, well-being, and consciousness.

As we travel through life, we must constantly examine whether each aspect of our inner matrix is aligned with our spiritual self. Once we develop that deep inner knowing, we can examine all that comes into our environment with a keen discernment about what we let into our field of consciousness and what we reject. With this increased awareness, we can conduct our lives in a very deliberate manner. Day by day, we continue to expand our connection to the spiritual until one day, this connection guides every thought, emotion, and action that we take.

When we step into conscious and focused action with the intention of love, peace, and compassion supporting us, we wield an infinitely powerful force to transform ourselves, our loved ones, and even the entire planet. No longer are we a mere pinball in a machine, bumping off the objects in our environment, reinforcing stagnant patterns of emotional destruction. Instead, we direct our thoughts, emotions, and physical sensations to align with what we wish to create.

With these skills, we gain the invaluable opportunity to play a critical role in the transformation of ourselves and others. We have the ability to serve as courageous leaders and forerunners perched on the horizon of change. We become agents of a desperately needed change at a critical time in our history. When we choose to step into this role, we give ourselves and all of humanity a priceless gift. We awaken from the illusion of separateness, step into our power to consciously create this world, and support humanity's remembrance of its divinity. This is the work of Conscious Transformation. This is the critical work we came to this planet to do. All that is required to achieve this level of majesty is that we have the courage to go within.

STRATEGY GUIDE:

Practices for Creating
Conscious Transformation

To consciously transform your life, the most important principle is consistency. Doing a practice every day is what empowers you to quickly change and create new patterns. Science has discovered that all it takes to rewire your brain is a daily twenty-minute mindfulness practice. Below you will find a nine-week mindfulness course along with exercises to assist you in increasing your level of awareness about how your inner matrix is currently wired and how to incorporate these Conscious Transformation practices into your life. These internal exercises are designed to bring about an increased level of awareness and focus to transform your mind, emotions, physical body and spiritual connection. The impact of these practices is profound. When you commit to daily practice, radical transformation will unfold as you become the architect of your life.

Daily Mindfulness Practice

Each week for nine weeks, there is a new daily mindfulness practice that applies the book's teachings of Conscious Transformation to shift and change your life. Pick a place to do your mindfulness practice every day. Although you can practice anywhere, I encourage selecting a quiet place where it is unlikely you will be interrupted. Arrange your space so that it invites contemplation. A comfortable chair where you can sit with your back straight or a cushion to sit on the floor is important. It is ideal but not required that you dedicate this space to your practice and resist doing other activities there. However, please know that I have students who have launched successful mindfulness practices from places such as their closet floor and even the front seat of their car.

If possible, commit to doing your practice at the same time every day. I routinely suggest to my students that they do the practice first thing in the morning or last thing at night. The most important element of success is consistently engaging the practice every day. If there are days when you cannot make your specified time, it is perfectly fine to move it, but having a set time to practice is of great support when beginning the work of Conscious Transformation. When your mindfulness practice is done in the same location and at the same time every day, your brain quickly begins to develop associations that support the practice. Your brain knows that at this time, every day, you sit in this place and practice for twenty minutes.

As you engage in certain activities in your daily life, your brain connects these circumstances with certain ways of being in the world. Knowing this, you can structure your mindfulness practice so the brain's love of pattern is at work for you. Think about when you drive to work in the morning. Is there a certain mental shift that takes place while you are en route? As you begin to transition from your personal to professional life, do aspects of a new persona emerge as you make the trip into your job? Are there changes in the quality of your thoughts, emotions and even your body? How about when you go to the gym? Before you arrive, does your heart rate increase a bit in anticipation of the work out? Routinely practicing in the same place and at the same time of day is just one small way that we can use the fact that the brain likes pattern to support our transformative work.

Checking In Practice

Exercises beyond a daily mindfulness practice are included to allow you to take these new skills deeper and shift your internal patterns at an accelerated rate. For each week, you will find a quick checking-in exercise to do throughout the day. By checking in on the state of your inner matrix, your mindfulness skills are incorporated into your daily life beyond your twenty-minute a day practice. Now you are not just *practicing*, you are *living* the work.

To check in, set an alarm on your computer, phone, or watch to go off in increments throughout the day. Once an hour is optimal. The more frequently you do the practices, the more rapid the changes will be. If you are at work and concerned about the noise, simply place your phone on vibrate or turn the sound of your alarm down low. When the alarm goes off, take just a moment to check into your internal state, using the tools that are provided. This practice takes only a minute or two but is a powerful tool for increasing awareness, interrupting your patterns, and bringing the benefit of Conscious Transformation into your daily life.

Journal Practice

For each week, there is also an exercise to allow you to further explore your inner matrix and gain new insights into how your inner matrix is wired. For these exercises, I suggest that you keep a journal to write down your reflections. Through these journaling practices, you will gain significantly greater awareness of the map of your inner matrix and how each aspect influences your experience of life. You should spend at least thirty minutes each week journaling, but remember: the more time you devote to these reflections, the greater the results. At various points in this work, we will ask you to look back to your writings and reflect on insights gained earlier in the practice. As a result, you will begin to have a clear picture of how deeply interconnected the patterns are in your mind, emotions, and physical body. Having these insights in writing will provide you with a map of your own inner matrix. You will find that these *awarenesses a*re invaluable on your path of transformation.

Creating Community

Although you can certainly do the work of Conscious Transformation on your own, having a community helps to facilitate your practice and support you on this journey. Starting a Conscious Transformation book club with family, friends, or coworkers is a great way to support your transformation and the transformation of those around you. It also allows you to share the work of Conscious Transformation with others and allow them to experience profound changes by reading the book and coming together each week for nine weeks of practice. My organization offers a variety of classes in Conscious Transformation for all who wish to be on a transformative path. Please check our website for upcoming programs at www.conscioustransformation.com.

The website provides a more in-depth version of this nine-week course, including recordings of the nine weeks of mindfulness practices, along with additional exercises to build and sustain your practice. Certified teachers are available to coach you through these practices and other Conscious Transformation practices. I encourage you to access our community and the tools we provide to support you in harnessing the power of your inner matrix to transform all aspects of your life.

As human beings, one of our deepest desires is for authentic connection to others. More and more, our culture has strayed from traditional systems that provided a sense of profound connection. Creating conscious connections with others who are on the path of evolving their level of consciousness offers the opportunity to form the type of truly intimate bond that has become all too rare in our society.

Nine-Week Practice Guide

Week 1—Increasing Awareness of the Inner Matrix and How It Drives You

Daily Mindfulness Practice: This week, you spend twenty minutes a day just being with yourself. Sit comfortably and close your eyes. Closing your eyes helps you to eliminate distractions from the outside world and to increase your sensitivity to what is occurring in your inner matrix. Focus on the state of your mind, emotions, and body. During that time, do not concentrate on the breath, listen to music, or use any techniques you may know for quieting the mind. Instead, just be mindful of whatever comes up during this time. Be aware of what thoughts, emotions, and physical sensations are present. Introduce yourself to you and establish a consistent daily practice. Do not judge what shows up. Just set the intention to be in a state of curiosity about what is present inside of you and take note of what is there.

Think about how you build a relationship with a new friend or lover. The first thing you do is spend time with that person to get to know them. In order to get to know yourself and see how your inner matrix is operating, you have to create a space to spend focused time with yourself. So in this first week, begin to create a daily mindfulness practice by sitting with yourself for twenty minutes a day. Even if you have been meditating for years, it always pays to spend quality time with yourself and just see where it takes you. No matter where you are on the path of transformation, there is always new awareness to have and higher levels of consciousness to reach. Remember, it is a good practice to use your journal to record *awarenesses* and experiences immediately after your mindfulness practice.

Check-In: During your first week, once an hour as you go about your day, stop what you are doing and take a moment to check in with what is occurring in your mind, body, and emotions. Ask yourself, *What is the mind thinking about? Are the thoughts of a higher or lower nature? Is the mind clear and focused or confused and chaotic? What emotions are present? Are they of a higher or lower nature? How does the body feel? What sensations am I experiencing in the body and where are those sensations located?*

Through checking in, you begin to create an awareness of how the inner matrix is driving behavior and creating your experience in the moment.

Journal: At the end of each day, take time to journal about what is showing up for you in the mind, emotions, and body. Reflect on your day. What are the consistent themes in each aspect of your inner matrix? Begin to look at what patterns are present for you. Are you thinking about the same people, places, things, or events over and over again? Take time and look at the mental, emotional, and physical patterns of which you are aware. Can you see how your inner matrix is creating the same experiences for you over and over again through these patterns?

In looking at the mind, ask what thoughts came up repeatedly? Were your thoughts primarily of a higher or lower caliber? Did you notice any reoccurring stories? Is your mind chaotic or organized? What emotional patterns were present for you? Were you aware of emotions triggering certain thoughts? Are you numb and shut down or are you joyful? What sensations did you notice in the body? Is your body tense or relaxed? Make note of any new awareness you gained from your daily check in. Journaling can be an important addition to the work of Conscious Transformation. When you take time to record insights, a true sense of clarity can begin to blossom.

Week 2—Increasing Focus of the Mind

Daily Mindfulness Practice: For twenty minutes a day, close your eyes and focus on *the four-sided breath.* To practice this breathing technique, sit up straight with the center of your head over the center of your pelvis. Sit comfortably either on the floor or in a chair. Place your tongue behind your front teeth, allowing it to rest against the roof or palate of the mouth. The four-sided breathing practice has four steps or *sides* to it. First, breathe a gentle inhale into your lower abdomen for three to four seconds while focusing on your center. Your center is located two inches below the belly button and an inch back toward the spine. Second, pause and hold your breath for a second or two. Third, exhale fully for three to four seconds. Fourth, pause and hold your breath for another second or two. Continuing to focus on your breath, repeat this four-sided breathing technique over and over again for twenty minutes.

If your mind drifts from focusing on the four-sided breath, gently acknowledge that the mind is thinking and simply redirect your focus back to the breath. Do not judge your level of focus, just simply return to the breath. This is critical. If your mind is busy criticizing, you are not focusing on the breath. Take note of where your mind went when you were not focused on the breath. Was it a to-do list? Your job? Someone special in your life? At times, your mind will drift away, but do not become discouraged or upset. At first, it can be hard to focus. The brain is like a muscle. You can think of the four-sided breathing practice as weight-lifting for the brain. Over time, you will get better. Focus is a skill that must be practiced if it is to be developed.

As you focus on the breath and still the mind, you begin to find your center and enter your natural states of well-being, which are peace, divine love, and joy. By centering yourself, you create a space where patterns that do not serve can be broken. In order to break or shift an internal pattern, we must first stop engaging the pattern by directing the mind elsewhere. Being able to focus the mind on the breath stops the train in its tracks and creates the space to focus on a new pattern that serves the vision you hold for your life.

Check-In: During the next week, as you go about your day, once an hour, check in with what is occurring in the mind, emotions, and body. Take time to simply acknowledge what is happening in your inner matrix. Then engage three or four cycles of the four-sided breath, and center yourself. Through this practice, you are developing the skill of being able to center yourself no matter what is going on around you. The four-sided breath allows you to disengage your patterns. Through this practice, you develop the ability to choose how you wish to show up. The beginning of living consciously is when you have the power to drive the mind instead of the mind driving you.

Journal: This week, journal about what you noticed when you checked in throughout your day. Note the lower thought patterns. Where did places of judgment show up? Were you aware of lower emotions fueling these lower thoughts and judgments such as anger, jealousy, unworthiness, shame, or guilt? Were you able to stop these mental and emotional patterns with the four-sided breath, or were they too strong to stop? If you couldn't stop the patterns completely, were you at least able to turn down their intensity? As you continued your practice, did it become easier to step out of the patterns? Were you able to find your center and shift into your natural state of peace, divine love or joy? Use this journaling time to get inside of exactly how your inner matrix is driving you and how you can step out of your conditioned patterns and into the higher state of your choosing. Begin to step into the power you can cultivate to control your mind.

Week 3—Mindfulness

Daily Mindfulness Practice: Initiate the same practice as last week, focusing on your center and breathing the four-sided breath. As a thought comes, just acknowledge the thought by saying to yourself, *My mind is thinking.* Envision a bright flame in the center of your forehead and drop the thought into the flame. Imagine the thought being burned by the flame. As the thought dissolves into smoke, focus on the space in between the thoughts. Enjoy that space of no thought. When the mind is still, a state of inner peace naturally surfaces from within.

Do not judge how long you are able to stay in the space between the thoughts. Entering this place of stillness is a skill that is developed with practice. As another thought emerges, simply repeat the exercise, acknowledging the thought, dropping it into the flame, and experiencing that space between the thoughts. This experience of peace is entered only in that space when the mind is still.

As thoughts arise, do not judge them. Thoughts are not good or bad. Thoughts are simply an expression of energy that our brain has been programmed to think. Remember that judgment causes the thoughts to become stronger. We simply cannot judge and be still at the same time. Eventually, we will develop the skill of replacing thoughts that do not serve with those that do, but for now, we must develop the ability to step out of judgment and step into the space between thoughts.

One of the benefits of developing this skill is that we become more aware of what our mind is thinking in our daily life. As a result we begin to see how we are creating our current reality and develop access to changing it. Eventually, the mind becomes like a light switch. We are moving to a place where the mind is no longer thinking us, instead, we are thinking the mind. As a result, we can begin to create the life we choose.

Check-In: When you check in this week, take a moment and be aware of your state of mind. Ask the question, *In this moment, is my mind aligned with love or fear?* Remember, there are only two energies in creation: love and fear. In any moment, your mind is either aligned with a state of love or a state of fear. It is impossible for your mind to align with both at the same time.

When you check in, if you notice that your mind is aligned with fear, use the four-sided breath to find your center and stop the fear-based thoughts and emotions. Then consciously focus the mind on a higher state and align yourself with divine love. Through this practice, you are developing the ability to focus on divine love, no matter what is happening in any moment.

Journal: Take time this week to develop awareness about how your current state of mind came to be. Your thoughts did not just show up one day. Instead, your mother, father, and early caregivers imprinted your thoughts, beliefs, and core concepts into your mind.

Journal about what you believe the environment was like when you were in your mother's womb. You were directly connected to your mother during this time, and you experienced all that she was experiencing. Was your mother's pregnancy planned? Was she in a supportive relationship with your father? Was she a member of a loving family, with close friends and a strong community? Was she alone and frightened? Was she working in a stressful environment at the time, or was she at home, preparing for your arrival? What was her financial condition? Take time to reflect on your mother's situation and to imagine all that she experienced while she was pregnant with you.

After you were born, you were in direct relationship with your external environment. Who was present in your environment during your early childhood years? Did you have a mother, father, grandparents, nannies, aunts, or uncles who cared for you and interacted with you frequently? What thoughts, beliefs, core concepts, and emotional patterns did they carry? What were your early caregivers experiencing during these years? What were their lives like? Were you in a loving and supportive environment or one layered with stress, tension, and anger? Spend time imagining what mental and emotional patterns were operating in those around you during your early childhood.

Who asserted a level of influence over your life? Did you have a teacher or mentor that supported you? Did this teacher or mentor mold your current way of thinking? What ideas did they plant inside of your mind? What thoughts, beliefs, core concepts, and emotional patterns did they carry?

As you do this work of seeing where your patterns came from, remember that your mother, father, early caregivers, and mentors did the best they could. They too were imprinted with mental and emotional patterns they did not choose. Although your mother, father, early caregivers, and mentors certainly had the best of intentions, no one can give a child what they do not have. Acknowledging where your patterns come from is beneficial in shifting and changing them. Spend time this week identifying as many mental and emotional patterns as you can and see clearly the connection to those who were caring for you at the beginning of your life. Take time to reflect on which of these mental and emotional patterns align with the life you intend to create and which do not support your vision.

Week 4—Emotional Awareness Practice

Daily Mindfulness Practice: Close your eyes, sit up straight, and begin thinking about the events of your day. If you are meditating in the morning, reflect on the events of the day before. Take ten minutes and focus on those situations that did not go as well as you would have liked. Look at those experiences where the strongest lower emotions showed up for you. Reflect on any lower emotional patterning around work, children, your partner, friends, family, or even strangers on the street. What situations triggered lower emotional patterns like anxiety, frustration, loneliness, anger, jealousy, unworthiness, abandonment, grief, depression, guilt, shame, disgust, despair, or sadness? As you reflect on each situation, silently name the emotion that was strongest for you in each experience. Through this practice, you increase your awareness of the lower emotional patterns that are most active during your day.

For the second ten minutes, focus on the emotion you identified that was the strongest during the first part of this practice. Do not think about the events and circumstances of the day that triggered the emotional pattern. Just be with the emotion. Set the intention to allow this lower emotion to fully express inside without resistance or reaction. Do not yell, tense the body, or react in any way. Instead, merely observe the emotion without judgment as it unfolds. When you feel the emotion strongly, say to yourself, *In this moment I am feeling* _____ and name the emotion that is present. Then affirm, *And that is okay.*

If you are working with one emotion and you notice another emotion emerge, repeat the process with this other emotion. For example, if you are working with anger and you notice sadness, do not focus on the mind; just allow sadness to fully express without resistance or judgment. Continue to repeat this process with each emotion that emerges until you find your center.

Once you find your center, enjoy your natural state of peace. If you aren't able to get there, do not judge the process. Just know that you will get there eventually. Remember, without thoughts to fuel an emotion, its life is only ninety seconds. Neurologically, an emotion can't last any longer unless you think about the situation that triggered it. If we are angry with loved ones and telling ourselves how horrible their actions are and why we are so justified in being angry with them, we can sustain anger for a long time. If on the other hand, we stop thinking and focus on the breath, anger can only sustain itself for a matter of seconds.

Through this exercise, you practice finding your center and accessing the peace that dwells within. Once you develop the ability to stop your thoughts, step out of lower emotions, and choose peace anytime you are triggered, the outside world can no longer control you. You are free.

Check-In: Every hour, tune in and ask yourself if you are aligned with love or fear this moment. What emotional state are you experiencing? Give a name to that emotion or feeling. When you have identified the emotion, say to yourself, *In this moment, I am feeling* _____ and name the emotion that is present. Then affirm, *And that is okay. It is a natural human expression.* Don't think about the situation triggering the emotion. Just be with the emotion without resistance or judgment until it dissolves. If it does not dissolve completely, use the four-sided breath to find your center and enjoy your natural state of peace.

Journal: Reflect on the emotions that are showing up throughout the day. What kinds of thoughts did the mind create in connection with each emotional pattern? Is it now apparent that the mind thinks in a particular way for each emotion? Identify which emotions are aligned with love and which are aligned with fear? When fear-based emotional patterns are present, such as sadness, anger, jealousy, unworthiness, anxiety, depression, or shame, what thoughts, beliefs, and concepts show up along with them? Start to notice how your emotion directs the mind to justify whatever emotional pattern is present. Are you beginning to recognize emotional patterns that are similar to those you identified as having been present in your mother, father, and early caregivers?

Set out the circumstances in which these emotional patterns have most frequently arisen and the impact they have had on your life. What place or places in your life are each of these emotions most active? For each emotional pattern, ask whether it is taking you closer to the vision you have for your life or further away from that vision? Step into a state of clarity about which emotional patterns serve your vision, which patterns do not serve, and which patterns you are committed to shifting and changing. Take time to record your insights in your journal.

Week 5—Shifting Emotion

Daily Mindfulness Practice: The first step in this week's practice is to identify one emotional pattern you can commit to shifting. For ten minutes, just be with that emotion without resistance or judgment. If you need to think about a situation in order to trigger an experience of the emotion, do so, but don't focus on the story for more than a minute or two. Then move out of those thoughts. Say to yourself, *In this moment, I am feeling* _____ and name the emotion, allowing it to fully express without reaction. Then affirm *and that is okay.* Allow the emotion to dissolve, and then move into your center, using the four-sided breath, if necessary.

For the next five minutes, select a higher emotional channel that you would like to embody, such as peace, divine love, or joy, and recall a state where you experience peace, divine love, or joy very intensely. If peace, divine love, and joy are not states that you remember experiencing on a deep level, then just imagine a situation where you would expect to experience one of these three states and envision how you would feel.

For the last five minutes, place your attention on a situation where a lower emotion has been present in the past. This time, imagine what it would be like to be in that same situation but in a higher emotional state. How would the situation unfold differently if peace, divine love, and joy were present instead of the lower emotion? For example, if the emotion you are working with is anger and you are reprimanded by your boss at work, can you see how stepping out of a place of anger and defensiveness would have changed how the situation unfolded? If you were able to hold a state of peace, divine love, or joy, can you imagine how the situation would look different? Would peace, divine love, or joy create an outcome closer to the vision you hold for your life more than anger would?

Remember, when you watch television, you are aware that the television program is a temporary experience. It is not who you are. If you don't like the program, you understand that you have the option to change the channel. You know you are not what is on the television screen. It is the same with emotions. You are not your emotions. Your emotions are merely a program, which you did not choose to create, that is running in your internal matrix. If you do not like the program, you can change the channel and pick a more pleasurable emotion. Because we can direct the mind, we have the power to focus on higher emotional expressions and acquire new ways of experiencing the world. For most, this power goes untapped. Through this practice, you will develop the skill of switching to a higher emotional channel anytime you choose.

Check-In: When you check in, ask yourself how you are feeling. Identify the emotion that is present and focus on allowing the emotion to fully express without resistance or judgment. Begin to breathe the four-sided breath and step into your center, focusing on the pattern you are committed to experiencing: peace, divine love, or joy. When you drop your thoughts and focus on your center, notice how peace, divine love, and joy expand. As you complete your checking-in exercise, set the intention to do your best to think, speak, feel, and take action from this higher state that you have chosen to embody.

Journal: Take time and reflect on the lower emotional state you are committed to shifting and changing in your life. Identify as many places as possible where that state shows up. In each situation, get inside exactly what experiences that emotional expression is creating. Can you see how this lower emotion is causing pain and suffering in your life? How is it creating more of the experiences you do not wish to have? What will your life look like in the future if this emotion continues to be present? What will your life look like if you step into peace, divine love, and joy and begin to take action from these states instead?

Now imagine being in situations where you experience a strong, lower emotion, such as those you identified the last two weeks. Imagine what it would be like to allow that lower emotion to express fully inside of you without reacting from that state. What would it be like to feel an emotion as fully as possible but not to be compelled to take action from it, swallow it, or cut yourself from it? Imagine what it would be like not to be caught in or controlled by the emotion. How empowering would it be to know that you could step out of a strong, lower emotion and choose the emotional state you wished to experience in any situation?

If you were to step out of lower emotions and step into your natural state of peace, divine love or joy, how would those situations you identified in your life be altered? Take time to look at each situation and imagine showing up in these high, natural expressions of peace, divine love, and joy. How would the condition of your mind change? Would you be able to access higher critical thinking from a state of peace as opposed to a state of anger? Would you feel less stress in your life? Would your health improve as a result? How would the world around you be reshaped if you were in a state of peace, divine love, or joy? Would you be making the type of contribution to the world that you have always desired?

Week 6—Physical Awareness of the Connection Between Mind and Body

Daily Mindfulness Practice: Every day for ten minutes, focus on the sensations that show up in your physical body. Start at the top of your head and slowly work your way all the way down to the tips of your toes. Cover your entire body, part by part, tuning into the sensations that you feel in each area. Pause at each different part of your body, and with curiosity, experience what is present. Ask *why* each sensation is there. Is the body relaxed or tight, tired or energetic, painful or pleasurable, hungry or satiated? What could be the underlying cause of each sensation? What is your body trying to communicate?

For the last ten minutes, start again at the top of the head, moving slowly through each area of the body. This time engage the four-sided breath. Focus and breathe the breath into each part of the body, one by one. Feel the body relax as the breath moves through it. Experience the stress and tension melting away with the breath. This is the body's natural state.

It is important to fully engage with this exercise, because you have been trained to ignore your body's communications. Instead of listening to what your body is trying to tell you, you have been taught to find ways to numb or overcome the symptoms instead of addressing the underlying issue that is present. If your body feels tired, society tells you to reach for caffeine instead of getting more rest. If your body aches, you were told to shake it off and trained to reach for ibuprofen, instead of looking to see what is causing that pain. Through this week's mindfulness practice, you can begin to undo that training and listen to your body again.

Check-In: In a quick form of the daily practice this week, take a couple of minutes to tune into the physical body each hour. What sensations are present? Ask yourself what the body is trying to communicate? Why is the body giving *this* communication? What is the underlying issue triggering the sensation? If you are tired, ask why that is? If your body is in pain, question what is causing it? Ask yourself how you can attend to the cause of the sensation instead of masking its symptoms. Ask what you can do to support your body. Finally, breathe a few cycles of the four-sided breath into the body and experience the body relaxing.

Journal: Reflect on what sensations you have noticed showing up in your body as you did your mindfulness practice and as you checked in throughout the week. Were there specific times and circumstances where you saw the same sensations showing up over and over again? Perhaps you were tired in the middle of the afternoon. Did you feel tension in your shoulders when you were at work? Was your energy low in the evenings when you were home with the kids?

Identify what sensations you are experiencing and what could be the underlying causes. Ask how you could take action to alleviate the underlying issues? Could you get more sleep? Work out more frequently? Drink more water? Eat a healthier diet? Focus your mind on finding answers that support your physical body to move into a state of optimal health and well-being.

Spend some time looking at how your life would change if you were in a state of higher energy and vibrancy? How would such a higher physical state impact the actions you took and the activities you engaged in? Would such a sense of optimal health and well-being influence your thoughts and emotions? Focus the mind on sensations, causes, solutions, and impact to bring clarity to how to best support your physical body.

Week 7—Creating a Vision for Your Body

Daily Mindfulness Practice: For twenty minutes a day, focus on the body, imagining what it would be like to embody a state of perfect health and well-being. Start at the top of your head and slowly move down the body, pausing at each different part until you reach the tips of your toes. For each body part, imagine what health, well-being and vibrancy would look like for that part. Imagine each and every part of your body in a state of pure perfection.

For each body part, offer gratitude and appreciation for all that it does. After all, it is the body that allows you to be on this planet and experience this life. Start with the brain. Affirm, *I am so grateful for my brain and how it allows me to be in the world, think higher thoughts, process all that is around me, and coordinate the function of my organs.* As you move down the body, make sure you are stopping to give gratitude for each organ, seeing every organ in a state of perfection.

As you move through the body, if you notice an ache or pain, stop, breathe into it and then go on with your work. This week, focus on being 100 percent grateful and appreciative of your miraculous body. Do not allow judgmental thoughts to intrude that do not support the vision you have for your body. Step out of any thoughts that criticize the body. This week focus on experiencing the body in a state of pure perfection.

Check-In: When you check in each hour this week, ask yourself what is going on physically, emotionally, and mentally. What emotions are tied to the sensations you are experiencing in the body. What thoughts are tied to these sensations? See how the thoughts and emotions impact the body. Look at how you are holding the body in the moment. Be aware of how your posture influences your thoughts and emotions. Breathe into those thoughts, emotions, and sensations and move into your natural state. As you do, align your body with your center. Sit up straight, open your chest, and drop your arms to your sides. The body's natural state is one with the spine aligned straight, jaw parallel to the ground, and heart open.

Journal: As you checked in this week, did you notice how thoughts and emotions shaped the state of your body? When certain emotions were present, what condition was your body in? How did your body feel in the presence of various lower emotions? What did you notice about the state of your body and its connection to certain types of thoughts you were having? When you were thinking lower thoughts, how did you hold your body? How did lower thoughts and emotions affect your posture? How did these lower patterns impact the level of stress in your body? Do you see a connection between how your body feels and the caliber of your thoughts and emotions?

The best way to shift the body is to tend to all levels of patterning at the same time. When we consciously drive the mind, shift the emotions, and take on a posture that aligns with our center, transformation occurs rapidly. Because these lower patterns get locked into the nervous system of our body, when we change the body to a state of strength and vibrancy, we are no longer supporting lower patterns in our thoughts and emotions. We can use the state of our body to support creation of the higher emotions and thoughts by being committed to training the body to facilitate and support our natural states of peace, divine love, and joy.

Week 8—Spiritual Awareness

Daily Mindfulness Practice: For twenty minutes each day, sit and tune into yourself. Ask what is unfolding for you in your mind, emotions, and physical body. Then focus on your four-sided breath. Breathe into your center and allow your natural state of peace, divine love, or joy to unfold. Now imagine a tube of light connected at the center of the heart and extending straight up out of the top of your head. Imagine following this tube of light out past your head, into the sky, out into outer space, and past the edge of our universe where the tube is connected to a presence of pure infinite energy. This infinite energy is unconditional or divine love. It is the source of energy that connects all beings. Imagine this space of unconditional love as a bright golden sun and begin to breathe your four-sided breath. Inhale this golden light in the form of pure, divine energy all the way down that tube and into your heart. Inhaling, draw infinite energy into the heart. Pause for a second or two. Exhaling, feel that light expand through the body. Pausing again, experience the energy anchoring in the body. Do this practice of breathing the four-sided breath from this place of unconditional love every day for twenty minutes.

Check-In: Stop and check into the overall patterns that are present for you in this moment. Ask yourself whether your mind, emotions, and physical body are aligned with fear or divine love? Connect to that infinite and unconditional love, and breathe that energy into any lower patterns that are present. Shift into patterns that serve you and breathe that divine love into the new patterns you wish to create.

Journal: This week, ask yourself where do I feel limited as I am living my day? What thoughts, emotions, and sensations are fueling or supporting this experience of limitation? What would my life look like if I were connected to this pure infinite energy throughout my day? How would these experiences of limitation shift? If I were connected to this pure infinite energy and I could manifest anything and create freely, what would I choose for my life? What vision would I create from this space of pure potential? What do I choose as my life's contribution to this world? Don't be afraid to dream big. Remember, you have unlimited power and potential supporting you. See your vision very clearly and spend time creating the details and experiencing what it would feel like to live your dream.

Week 9—Transcending the Thoughts, Emotions, and Physical Body

Daily Mindfulness Practice: Sit for twenty minutes a day and create a vision for your life. See yourself ten years from now and create any vision for your life that you choose. Ask yourself what thoughts, emotions, and physical sensations would align with that vision. Choose a vision that you feel passionate about and make certain that your vision aligns with a state of divine love. Now connect to that state of divine love. In that place of infinite, pure Presence, see yourself living that vision. Imagine yourself having mental, emotional, physical, and spiritual experiences that support your vision. Drop any doubt. Step into awareness that anything is possible when you create from this space of pure, infinite energy. Experience being in your vision, and allow it to fully unfold.

Check-In: Every hour, check into what is present in your thoughts, emotions, and physical body. *Am I aligning my inner matrix with the vision I have for my life? Am I connected to that space of unconditional divine love?* If not, connect to that pure Presence and use the tools and techniques you have now learned to align your thoughts, emotions, and physical body with your long-term vision. Breathe from that space of divine love.

Journal: As you are creating your vision through your mindfulness practice and checking-in exercises, journal each day to support your creation. If you could do anything with absolutely no restriction from money, time, or ability, what would you create? Discover where your passion lies. Get inside the details of your vision. See yourself living that vision. Identify the thoughts, emotions, and physical embodiments that align with your long-term vision. Now see mind, emotions, and physical body all in alignment with your vision. When you are living this vision, what level of spiritual connection is present? See yourself experiencing the thoughts, emotions, sensations, and spiritual connections that are necessary to create your vision. See yourself consciously choosing the states in your mind, emotions, and physical body that support your vision. See yourself consciously transformed.

ABOUT THE AUTHOR

Joey Klein is the founder of Conscious Transformation, a cutting-edge system that teaches people to transform their lives using the practices he developed and has used during years of study with gifted spiritual teachers from around the world. He leads classes and retreats that focus on changing core mental, emotional and physical patterns to enrich and enhance daily life, deepening the connection to spirit. He is a three-time world martial arts champion and sought-after speaker whose writings, teachings and interviews have been published in fourteen countries. For over a decade, his work has brought profound transformation to thousands of lives. He currently lives in Vail, Colorado.

CPSIA information can be obtained
at www.ICGtesting.com
Printed in the USA
LVOW03s0555290617
539727LV00001BD/1/P